W9-BIH-585

fearless
in the kitchen

christine cushing

fearless in the kitchen

innovative recipes
for the uninhibited cook

VIKING
CANADA

VIKING CANADA

Published by the Penguin Group

Penguin Books, a division of Pearson Canada, 10 Alcorn Avenue, Toronto, Ontario, Canada M4V 3B2

Penguin Books Ltd, 80 Strand, London WC2R ORL, England

Penguin Putnam Inc., 375 Hudson Street, New York, New York 10014, U.S.A.

Penguin Books Australia Ltd, 250 Camberwell Road, Camberwell, Victoria 3124, Australia

Penguin Books India (P) Ltd, 11, Community Centre, Panchsheel Park, New Delhi – 110 017, India

Penguin Books (NZ) Ltd, cnr Rosedale and Airborne Roads, Albany, Auckland 1310, New Zealand

Penguin Books (South Africa) (Pty) Ltd, 24 Sturdee Avenue, Rosebank 2196, South Africa

Penguin Books Ltd, Registered Offices: 80 Strand, London WC2R ORL, England

First published 2002

10 9 8 7 6 5 4 3

Copyright © Christine Cushing, 2002
Colour photography © Per Kristiansen, 2002
Black and white photography © Lorella Zanetti, 2002

All rights reserved. Without limiting the rights under copyright reserved above, no part of this publication may be reproduced, stored in or introduced into a retrieval system, or transmitted in any form or by any means (electronic, mechanical, photocopying, recording or otherwise), without the prior written permission of both the copyright owner and the above publisher of this book.

Printed and bound in Canada on acid-free paper.
Manufactured in Canada.

NATIONAL LIBRARY OF CANADA CATALOGUING IN PUBLICATION DATA

Cushing, Christine
    Fearless in the kitchen : innovative recipes for the uninhibited cook / Christine Cushing.

Includes index.
ISBN 0-670-04334-6

1. Cookery. I. Title.

TX715.6.C88 2002   641.5   C2002-903872-3

Visit Penguin Books' website at **www.penguin.ca**

contents

detailed contents

essentials 83

simply irresistible 109

I dare you! 139

sweet science 165

index 199

acknowledgements

There are many people to thank for making this book possible:

My editor, Nicole de Montbrun, for having faith in me and searching high and low for the perfect book title.

KitchenAid Canada — in particular Eric Bauchet — for making the beautiful photos happen and for his continued support.

Everyone at Pusateri's, for providing me with the absolute best products a chef could dream of. Pusateri's has truly been an inspiration to me from the first time I walked through the door. I'm thinking of adding my own wing to the back so I don't have to commute.

My family, who continue to support me no matter how insane things get.

My husband, for putting up with countless bodies traipsing in and out of our kitchen to develop the recipes.

Juan Salinas, my sous chef and great friend, for all his help and guidance with the recipe development.

Dana Spears, for all her tireless efforts with the recipes and editing. I'm glad she moved from New York.

Josie Malevich, for her patience and expertise in compiling, organizing and going through all those food quizzes and recipes. I couldn't have done it without you.

Per Kristiansen, for his awesome food shots and for a truly fearless cover. I think we make a great team! You went above and beyond the call of duty.

Lorella Zanetti, for changing the meaning of a one-day shoot. Your eye for detail and continued quest for perfection have made the black-and-white shots in the book something out of an Italian fashion magazine. Who says you can't do your best work three weeks before giving birth? Lorella, you can take my picture anytime, anyplace.

Mary Opper, for a great sleek book design and for keeping things simple and loose.

John Lettieri, for providing us with not only a great location to shoot our photos but a few great faces to boot. You never cease to amaze me.

My producer Krista Look, for always being there for me for everything from wardrobe to reorganizing my kitchen. There are really no words to describe my gratitude.

My team from *Christine Cushing Live*, for listening to my rants, especially Theresa Kowall Shipp and James Smith. You guys all rock!

The Food Network, for believing in me and giving me such a great platform to springboard from.

Everyone at Penguin Books who worked so hard and will continue to do so after the book hits the shelves.

Everyone who filled out the quizzes, and Dan, Joe, Rob, Marci and Laura for sharing their cooking philosophies with me.

introduction

After many years of cooking for myself, clients, family and friends and developing recipes for magazines and television shows, I have come to the conclusion that my favourite part of cooking is the spontaneous excitement of creating an absolutely earth-shattering dish.

When I used to cater, my favourite clients were the ones who said to me, "Christine, this is how much money we have in the budget and this is what we can't eat. Go crazy and have fun." Keeping my options wide open, not having the slightest clue exactly what I was going to cook until the day of the event, made the process much more exciting. I found I did my best creative work when I had just a rough idea of what I was going to prepare. I would trot off to the market and seek inspiration from what was available. My senses would overload, and then maybe a smell or a colour or a new ingredient would trigger an idea and the menu would come together. Although this fearless approach to catering isn't the most practical, for me it is the most exhilarating. Nowadays, when I have to be prepared in advance with the recipes for television, I feel so restricted!

Having to work out the specifics of a recipe and testing and retesting the recipe until it was perfect led me to wonder about personal styles of cooking. Who follows recipes and why? How linked are habit and personality to the way we cook? I wanted to know who else was fearless in the kitchen and who wasn't.

Perhaps the secret really is in our personality. Maybe people who live every moment passionately cook with that same reckless abandon. Maybe those who weigh every move logically in their everyday affairs are more inclined to weigh and measure their ingredients carefully. Maybe those who cook out of necessity, who have to cook every day whether they want to or not, view cooking as one more chore. Perhaps they follow a recipe to make cooking easier and less fussy. Maybe those who don't get any creative release during the day's grind can't wait to get home and cook because the kitchen is their playground.

My main reason for writing this book is for some of my fearlessness in the kitchen to rub off on you. The recipes in this book truly reflect my personal style of cooking, featuring unusual ingredients and all kinds of ethnic inspirations, because I think food should never be boring. As a general rule, the further you go into the book, the more innovate and challenging the recipes are. But I want you to have fun with this book and try recipes from all the chapters, be they simple or more difficult.

I also feel strongly that food shouldn't be overly complex. I have noticed that over the years my style of cooking has streamlined and simplified, and I keep making adjustments. I am never afraid to experiment or to explore new culinary frontiers. (Sounds like a *Star Trek* episode!) That's how I stay inspired and fearless.

I am fearless. Well ... except for the time someone tried to get me to eat durian fruit. I don't care how much of a delicacy the durian is, but when there are signs on buses in Thailand forbidding you to take durian on board because they absolutely, for lack of another word, stink, I'm not eating them! Sorry, I can't get past the smell. But hey — I tried! As you go through the book and prepare the recipes, all I ask is that you *try* to make little changes to interpret them your way, *try* a substitution or a new ingredient — that's the key to being fearless in the kitchen.

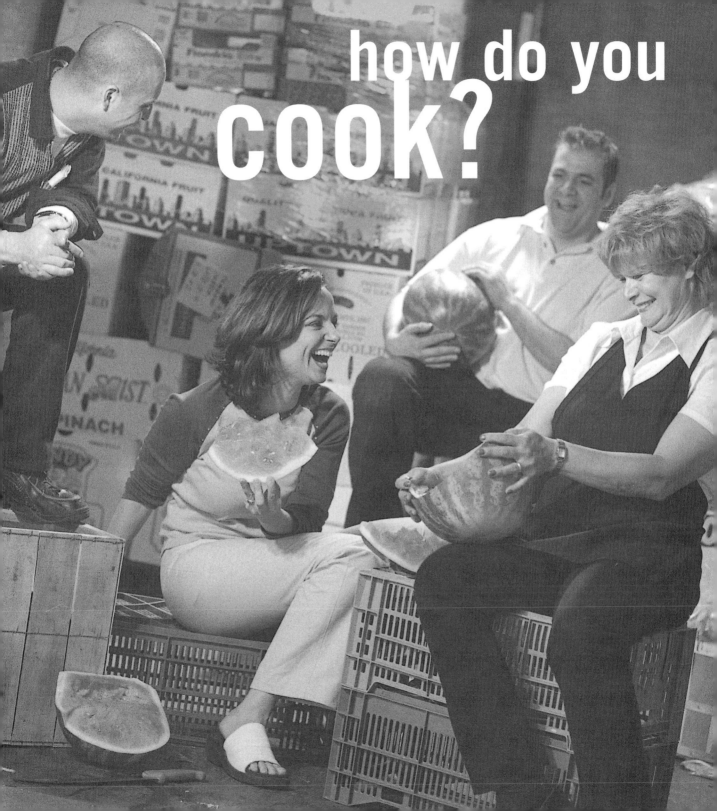

I took some time to observe,
probe and question the wa
my family, friends, associates
and neighbours cook an
I'm sharing it with you.
I devised a quiz that is a great wa
to observe patterns of the way we cook,
but the play by play really tells the story of
who is fearless in the kitchen
The kitchen is full of real stories,
and here are just a few,
including my own.

how do you cook?

It's a fact: we all cook differently and use recipes in our own unique ways. When I cook, I like to keep my options wide open. Even *I* don't know exactly how it's going to turn out until it hits the plate. I let my senses and my imagination guide me. I think I'm pretty fearless. How do you cook? Do you follow a recipe to the letter, or are you just as comfortable "winging it"? Are you flustered if you discover that you don't have the right ingredients on hand? Do you carefully measure each ingredient, or do you cook by "feel"?

Thinking about these questions led me to devise a quiz to try to find out whether there was some pattern among people who follow recipes and those who don't. You'll find my cool little quiz and my findings later in this chapter. Take the quiz. Are you fearless in the kitchen? Give it to your friends. Are they fearless in the kitchen? The quiz is a fun little tool to try to establish patterns in our cooking behaviour. There are no right or wrong answers. Your score will not prevent you from successfully cooking any recipe anywhere in this book. If your score tells you that you could take a few more risks in the kitchen, then you might want to read through chapter 2 a little more closely for advice on interesting ingredients, substitutions and how I approach a recipe.

I'd like to encourage those of you who rely closely on a recipe to try a small variation after you've perfected the recipe. Maybe those of you who feel confident and love playing in the kitchen can take the ultimate risk: find a recipe in the book that sounds irresistible, then follow the ingredients and the method but ignore the measurements — follow your own instinct.

When I started to cook, I rarely used any measures. When I went to cooking school, however, that came to an abrupt stop because I had to execute the recipe exactly as it was written or the chef-instructor would freak. But when I (begrudgingly) followed the measurements and instructions, I found that I could concentrate on, and perfect, my technique. Later, when I began to write recipes, this training proved invaluable. I found I could imagine a recipe in my head and write it down as though I was cooking it. Now writing recipes has become one of my best skills, even though when I cook there is no recipe in sight (unless, of course, I'm baking).

I can tell you that I rarely make a dish exactly the same way twice, but that's just me. I don't expect you to start changing the recipe for no reason. I mostly want you to explore more options — and keep it fun.

what is your cooking personality?

Personality does sway cooking styles to some degree — it has to. There are extremes in personalities: the typically A personality (A for anal and angst) and the typically B personality (B for bold and brash).

Type A's in the kitchen stick to their shopping lists and don't give in to impulse buys, and they have to have things just so ("Why are you doing that? The recipe says to do this — you can't do that"). They measure each ingredient exactly and follow the recipe to the letter. There are also the extreme type B's who are lax and spontaneous in the kitchen and not fazed by any setbacks or forgotten ingredients (and they usually do forget things because they don't have a list, so they are inherent problem solvers because they have to be). They don't measure, they just wing it ("That's not enough; I'm adding way more than that").

But more often than not most people are blends of type A and B in different situations and arenas. They have personalities somewhere in the middle, with a slight pull to A or B. Some have a more inherently scientific view, while others have a more artistic/creative view. So type A, who can't factor in the senses (tasting, smelling, seeing, touching, hearing) or instinct or can't problem-solve setbacks, doesn't do well in the kitchen, because often cooking is not a constant — there are so many factors that come into play, such as the weather, oven temperature, quality of an ingredient, interpretation of recipe directions. Similarly, type B may fail in the kitchen when baking or when specific ratios are called for or an understanding of flavour principles is needed, because baking and some cooking does depend more on science and measuring.

People who are really fearless in the kitchen usually have a good mix of both A and B. It isn't all or nothing, and one type is not worse than another. For instance, it's a benefit to be anal and specific about the quality of your ingredients and about balancing flavours, and of course precise timing can be important in the kitchen as well.

So a really good fearless cook has an instinct about cooking and a basic understanding of the principles and methods of cooking and baking. This person likes a challenge and is drawn to tasks where they are discovering, exploring, learning, problem-solving and being creative. There is a lot of hard work in cooking, and for many people who are fearless in the kitchen, it is not comments and praise about their cooking that they seek but that personal satisfaction from discovering and creating. There are so many things to learn about in cooking, and exploring creates true fearlessness.

Of course the more you cook different things, the more understanding and more experience you will have. But how you view cooking (and how you define yourself) affects your cooking style. If you're convinced that cooking is a chore and isn't worth the effort and you prefer to have a bowl of cereal or fast food for dinner instead of making something special for yourself or others, well, chances are you do not consider yourself fearless in the kitchen. If you don't think you are very creative or artistic, then you may never venture into the kitchen and experiment.

I'm suggesting that you take small steps to experience the world of fearlessness. It takes a bit of practice, but it can be very invigorating. I had to do the reverse in order to perfect making pastry. I started by throwing things in a bowl but eventually I taught myself to become more disciplined and measure exact quantities to yield perfect pastry results. Herbs, spices and sauces are great to start improvising with until you feel comfortable.

If you try a little substitution of your own and you don't like it, try something slightly different the next time you make the dish, until you have a meal you love. You may find yourself becoming addicted to making your own adjustments to recipes. There are no "mistakes" in the fearless kitchen.

So, time for that quiz. I'll give you my analysis of the answers I got afterwards (just so their results don't influence you). Everyone who took the quiz was a home cook, and the interviews that follow are also with everyday people who cook at home, for friends or just for the heck of it.

I have to confess that I had my preconceived notions of how people would cook just based on their personalities. I wasn't always right, but usually the loudmouthed, outgoing types (like me!) were less structured in their cooking.

are you fearless in the kitchen?

1. When you cook, is it
   A. mostly a chore?
   B. sometimes a chore and sometimes a joy?
   C. mostly a joy?

2. Which do you prefer?
   A. Baking.
   B. Cooking.
   C. No preference, enjoy both.

3. When you grocery shop, do you have a list?
   A. Almost always.
   B. Sometimes.
   C. Almost never.

4. When you grocery shop, you buy a cart of food items that
   A. is almost the same every week.
   B. varies somewhat every week.
   C. varies significantly every week.

5. On average, do you use a recipe
   A. as a law?
   B. as a guide?
   C. as a springboard for ideas?

6. When cooking a favourite recipe, you
    A. make it exactly the same way every time.
    B. vary it a bit each time.
    C. almost never cook the same recipe twice.

7. For you, what is "experimenting in the kitchen"?
    A. Trying a new recipe.
    B. Trying to improve a recipe with your own twist.
    C. Creating a new dish without a recipe as a guide.

8. When you can't find a major ingredient called for in the recipe, what do you do?
    A. Keep shopping, because you have to have the right ingredient or you can't make the dish.
    B. Substitute with an ingredient you have.
    C. Substitute with an ingredient you have and start to change the recipe even more.

9. When the recipe calls for 1 tsp. of oregano, you
    A. get out the measuring spoons.
    B. estimate what 1 tsp. looks like.
    C. use an amount of oregano to your own taste.

10. Which best describes your views on cooking?
    A. Cooking is more science than art.
    B. Cooking is equal parts science and art.
    C. Cooking is more art than science.

your fearless score

For each A answer, give yourself 1 point.

For each B answer, give yourself 5 points.

For each C answer, give yourself 10 points.

for scores between 10 and 40, you are reluctant to be fearless in the kitchen

PROFILE

You are fearful and careful in the kitchen and follow instructions to the letter.

ADVICE

Try to use the five senses more in the kitchen: smell and taste as you go along. Take baby steps to becoming more fearless in the kitchen. Try to vary a recipe by substituting an ingredient or two. Try to worry less about measuring and instead season to your own taste.

for scores between 41 and 60, you are hesitant to be fearless in the kitchen

PROFILE

You are a little hesitant in the kitchen but you do "break the rules" now and again. When cooking, you are not frazzled by minor setbacks but you can still get stressed. You can adapt and use your senses but you need much more confidence to become more fearless in the kitchen.

ADVICE

Try to experiment a little more. Buy an ingredient that you have never used before. Cook it simply and don't fuss with it to see what it tastes like, and if you like it, cook it again with something that you think it would go well with.

for scores between 61 and 74, you are almost fearless in the kitchen

PROFILE

You almost always feel relaxed and confident in the kitchen. You are not afraid to try new recipes and buy new ingredients, but you need that extra push to create dishes that have your very own signature.

ADVICE

Try to create your own recipe without using a cookbook as a guide. Go to the grocery store and just pick some fun ingredients and try to make a dish that is your very own. Experiment. Experiment. Experiment!

for scores between 75 and 100, you are fearless in the kitchen

PROFILE

You feel relaxed and content in the kitchen. You love cooking, and it comes naturally to you. You can probably create a dish from some pantry items that would impress a crowd.

ADVICE

Share your fearlessness and your masterpieces with others!

how to be more fearless in the kitchen

- Buy a new ingredient that intrigues you from my favourite fearless ingredients listed in chapter 2 and find a recipe that uses it. Experiment with it in a dish you already make that you think it would work well with.
- When you eat out, order something you've never tried before. This is a way of expanding your knowledge of flavours and the way they work together. Try to recreate at home the flavours or dishes you enjoy. Don't be afraid to ask the servers if you can't figure out what some ingredients or flavours are.
- Create an environment that is comfortable for cooking in — listen to your favourite music or have a glass of wine. I find I cook best with the stereo blasting. It seems to give me inspiration.
- Get the senses going in the kitchen. Smell and taste and feel and watch and listen as you cook.
- Don't treat cooking as a chore, treat it as entertainment, enjoyment, meditation, learning, discovery, a creative outlet. Cook with friends. Take a cooking class, on your own or with some friends; treat it as entertainment and have fun.
- Learn and practise the cooking basics and build your confidence. Cook from basic recipes to help you learn basic techniques and ratios, then start building on your knowledge by experimenting.

background information

Here are the background questions that I asked each person who filled out the quiz so I could analyze the results better.

1. Sex
   A. male
   B. female

2. Age
   A. 20 years or younger
   B. 21–35 years

C. 36–50 years

D. 51–65 years

E. 66 years or older

3. Occupation _____

4. Do you balance your chequebook?

    A. All the time.

    B. Most of the time.

    C. Sometimes.

    D. Almost never.

5. Can you leave the house without having a destination?

    A. Why would I do that?

    B. I guess I could.

    C. Sometimes.

    D. Where am I now?

6. When you are at home, your keys are

    A. in the same spot every time.

    B. in one of three places.

    C. somewhere in the house.

    D. My keys, my keys, where are my keys?

7. When you are trying to make an important decision, you

    A. analyze the pros and cons.

    B. analyze the pros and cons but factor in your gut instinct.

    C. just follow your gut instinct.

8. Do you cook for children and/or teenagers?

    A. No.

    B. Yes, under 5 years.

    C. Yes, between 6 and 12 years.

    D. Yes, between 13 and 18 years.

quiz results

I got back 91 completed quizzes. I heard from 59 women and 32 men. (It turned out to be far easier to get a quiz back from a woman than from a man ... but I don't want to analyze this!)

I was hoping that the results would show that those who balance their chequebook all the time, know where their keys are all the time and always have a destination when they leave the house would have a low fearless score. But when I compared the ten lowest scores with the ten highest scores, there was no clear match in personalities, except for the fact that 50% of the lowest scorers answered "why would I leave the house without a destination?" and 40% of the high scorers said that they sometimes leave the house without a destination.

low fearless score	high fearless score
60% almost never balanced their chequebook	40% balanced their chequebook all the time
60% knew where their keys were	60% also knew where their keys were

sex

There were no definitive, mind-shattering differences between men and women, but there were some subtle differences. I found that women were just slightly more fearless than men, even when they had similar occupations. Men averaged a score of 48 and women averaged 55. Eight of the ten highest scores were women, and six of the ten lowest scores were men. The highest score for a man was 76 and the highest score for a woman was 90. The lowest score for a man was 14 and the lowest score for a woman was 22.

men	women
Use a little less instinct in cooking; that is, they measure more and are less likely to add an ingredient to their own taste	Fewer women get out the measuring spoons and they more freely add to their own taste
Slightly more men than women believe that cooking is more science than art	Slightly more women than men said that cooking is more art than science (A majority of men and women said it is equal parts science and art.)
Slightly more men than women said that they buy the same cart of groceries week to week (they also like their keys in the same spot)	Slightly more women than men prefer baking, but a higher percentage of women enjoy both baking and cooking

occupation

When sorted by occupations, the quiz scores were usually similar or within the same range, especially when the occupations were similar or more specialized. For instance, there were musicians, graphic artists, architects, executives, marketing managers, police officers, teachers, business analysts, techies and TV producers who scored exactly the same or closely in the same range. There were wide ranges in managerial, sales and administrative positions.

The ten lowest scorers included three police officers, two managers, two exec types, one stay-at-home mom/bookkeeper, one principal and one teacher. The ten highest scorers were two architects, one sales coordinator, one retail account rep, one admin assistant, one customs specialist, one publicist, one housewife, one manager and one microbiologist technician.

Obviously, career influences the way we cook. Professions with highly specific, regimented routines seem to yield cooks who need to follow the rules. Conversely, those who are in more creative jobs seem to use that creativity in the kitchen.

A great way to increase your fearlessness in the kitchen is to cook with someone who works in a field completely different from your own. For example, if you're a book-keeper, try making dinner with a salesperson. The two of you will probably drive each other crazy in the kitchen, but you will pick up techniques from the opposite end of the spectrum. (You may want to invite a mediator, just in case.)

age

There was no correlation between fearlessness and age.

interviews

I thought my quiz was a great way to find patterns in the way we cook, but the real-life play by play is what really tells the story of who is fearless in the kitchen. I spent some time observing my friends, associates, neighbours — even some strangers! — at work in the kitchen. Here are just a few examples to show what it takes to be truly fearless in the kitchen.

dan

(Late 20s; newspaper production)

Dan has only just begun his journey in cooking and watches many of the shows on the Food Network. Since he's not quite confident enough yet, he always begins with a recipe and always shops with a list. But when he gets home from the grocery store, he invariably realizes that he forgot to get half his ingredients. He hesitates to substitute other ingredients, and so begins his ritual of playing the "call a friend" card. One friend's advice is never sufficient, so he has multiple calls going to ensure that he's heading in roughly the right direction. He's not a very trusting fellow, is he?

Then the apron goes on, along with the radio. Dan has to absolutely use measuring utensils. After his second reading of the recipe, he still doesn't quite get the instructions and thinks he needs the "kindergarten equivalent." It's possible he's overambitious in his recipe selection.

After he swears to following the recipe directions the first time, he goes off on the journey to improve the dish. Not bad for a beginner. The thing that keeps him going is his love of cooking. He'll cope with missing ingredients and struggle with unclear directions and even bad advice because he just loves to cook. He admits that his girlfriend is a better cook then he, but also that he'll cook for her more often than she'll cook for him. When asked if he ever cooks without a recipe, Dan says, "I usually hide it under something so it looks like I know what I'm doing."

In my books Dan is definitely on the road to being fearless in the kitchen. Give him a few years and he'll be sailing through those recipes because of his unrelenting love for the kitchen. Dan's caution and dependence on the recipe may result from inexperience now, but what he's learning will prove priceless.

marci

(Late 20s; steelworker)

Marci gave off a very interesting vibe when we started talking about cooking because she has two completely distinct approaches, depending on whether she is cooking for herself or for friends. Marci says that after working a 12-hour shift she hardly feels like cooking. (Understandable.) She'll usually go shopping without a list, pick out whatever, and make a simple chicken breast supper. She never uses or even consults a recipe. Instead she seems to have a circuit of about five different ways she'll make chicken. It's never exactly the same way twice.

But when Marci is having friends over, her approach is totally different. She starts with a recipe, from which she will always write a list. She executes the recipe with a very organized approach and cleans up as she goes along. She tends to follow the recipe verbatim. Marci says, "If it's in the book, it's got to be right!"

The other thing I find interesting about Marci's cooking adventures is that she never cooks the same recipe twice for friends. Once she's made a recipe, she puts it in her memory bank and it goes into the "cook for self" roster. And when she makes it for herself, she does not consult that recipe again. Next time she has friends over, she picks a new recipe and follows it to a T.

Marci seems to feel that cooking for herself is a chore but cooking for others is a joy. I'm sure many of us can relate. I see many signs of a fearless cook in Marci, but when she's cooking for guests — when it counts — she wants to know that she's following the sound professional advice of a recipe.

joe

(Early 30s; contractor)

Joe loves cooking for friends and he always builds a menu after asking what they don't like. Then, he says, "I like to introduce them to something they may not have had." Clearly Joe's philosophy is very interactive, and he wants his guests to enjoy every minute of their dinner. With all the philosophizing behind him, Joe sets about finding his recipe. He usually consults one but then interprets it his way. "I kick it up a notch."

With shopping list in hand, Joe peruses the aisles and looks for further inspiration. He makes a habit of talking to the staff and telling them what he intends to cook. He doesn't want to take their advice, though — he just wants to talk. If he can't find an ingredient, he just substitutes whatever he feels like.

Once back in the kitchen, he begins an organized approach to cooking dinner. The original recipe may be somewhere in the kitchen to glance at, but it's usually consigned to memory. Joe may jot down a few notes on the recipe about how he's going to adapt or change it. He's cooking it his way no matter what.

Joe is definitely fearless. He's going to have fun cooking, he's going to use the recipe as a basic guideline and he loves using new ingredients. I have one question for Joe: "When are you going to cook me dinner?"

rob

(Late 20s; deli manager, gourmet shop)

Rob's answer to "How do you use recipes?" is, "Recipes ... are you kidding me? I never use recipes. I try to pick foods that complement each other well." At least he's got some kind of plan.

Rob likes to use other people's knowledge (i.e., chefs) but he never does what they tell him. He also says he never takes a list when he shops; instead, he walks through the stores with a basic idea of what he's going to make and hopes to be inspired. For example, if he was going to use zucchini but today's Portobello mushrooms look amazing, he'll just pass by the zukes and pick up those plump Portobellos instead. While he's shopping he is also thinking of what wine he'll serve.

When I was interviewing him, Rob was cooking for his friend's birthday dinner and he was elated at the fruits of his labour. The dinner began with a roasted Portobello appetizer smothered with tapenade and topped with a sharp goat cheese. (Now remember, there's not a recipe to be seen anywhere, so he followed his instinct when it came to quantities and methods.) He emphasized many times, "If you don't follow your gut, you're ..." You fill in the blank.

When I asked him, "What if something goes wrong?" Rob replied, "You just fix it. How would anyone know you made a mistake?" He's obviously a problem solver and thrives on the rush of righting a wrong. Everyone loved his dinner, and Rob admits that the most important thing for him is for the visual element of the food to balance the taste. "When the food can taste as great as it looks, then you know you've done a great job. Oh, and if everyone leaves the dinner table with a smile on their face, I feel great."

No doubt in my mind, Rob is not only fearless but he wants to start his own culinary galaxy. He doesn't follow recipes, he lets the available ingredients inspire him and he follows his gut. Moreover, he loves to cook for people, when he can go all out.

laura

(Late 30s; photographer)

Laura's dinner plans always begin with the ever important recipe selection. She wants the best-quality ingredients and she will travel miles to get them. When asked about how much she relies on the recipe, Laura admitted that she treats it as gospel and doesn't stray from the plan unless forced to. (I'm thinking that either a sign from God or a phone call from Martha Stewart would be the only two ways she'd change a recipe.) She did say, though, that if she's shopping in a hurry she may just leave something out if she hasn't found it in a couple of places.

She also puts all her efforts into the main course because she thinks that's what dinner hinges on. She says the appetizer and dessert "are not as crucial." So far Laura's cooking style reflects her vocation, since photographers have to be very precise with their light readings and exposures.

The first thing she does when she gets home from shopping is perch the recipe on the counter so she can see it at all times. And she follows the recipe to the letter. In fact, if something appears to go wrong, she will pitch the whole lot and start from scratch. (She told me about a time when she made Cornish hens with grapes and she thought they were lousy, so she went back to the grocery store, bought chicken breasts and made dinner all over again.)

It's obvious that Laura is a believer that cooking is a true science and should not be messed with. It could also be that she still doesn't feel comfortable enough in the kitchen to take some chances. I think she definitely appreciates the innovation of a great new dish, but her idea of being fearless would be to try a new recipe exactly the way it's written on paper. (Not that there's anything wrong with that.)

As Laura chooses recipes in this book, she'll probably mark her favourites and keep coming back to them. Her adventure may be to try some of the more complex recipes in the back of the book as well as to try some new ingredients. Whatever she chooses to cook, I know she'll do a great job. I've been to her place for dinner and it's always fantastic.

You are going to need a little technical help to get started. I'll begin by describing my approach to recipes. Then I'll run through **the cooking terms** you'll often see, provide theory and tips on substitutions, list **my top spices** and **share** how I use herbs. I'll also describe my favourite ingredients, including a list of flavour boosters. **Experiment** to find your own favourites.

breaking free from the recipe

Why do so many of us get hung up on specific quantities in a recipe? We fret, "How much is a dash? Is my pinch bigger than yours?" Here's my answer: in the big scheme of things, civilizations won't collapse because you added too much hot sauce to your chili or you doubled the basil in the pasta sauce. If you don't like it, you can always make adjustments the next time. As a rule, it's easier to add a little something than to take it away, so I recommend starting out slowly — add a touch here and there as the flavour begins to develop.

Following a recipe exactly is a great way to learn — and it gives you a reliable jumping-off point. But I think following the recipe exactly the same way every single time is boring (yes, even my own recipes!). Besides, it creates a dependency on some-one else's taste. Just because I like three sprigs of thyme on my roast chicken doesn't mean you should be obligated to follow suit. Maybe you hate thyme, or maybe you can never get enough. (I exclude baking recipes from this free-hand approach. I'll tackle that beast in the dessert chapter.)

So how should we view a recipe? Is it simply a guideline or is it etched in stone? I think that feeling obligated to follow a recipe precisely the same way every time is like riding your bike all your life with the training wheels on. When you begin to learn to ride a bike, it's great to know those little wheels are there to prevent you from falling flat on your face. But once you've got down the basics of how to pedal and steer, the training wheels can come off. And then you're free to fly anywhere you want, in your own style, at your own pace, and head off on your own adventures.

I want this book to inspire you to get out of the safety zone, once you feel comfort-able with your fundamental cooking skills. That's the key to being an uninhibited, fearless cook.

I think there should always be an element of surprise in the kitchen, and to a degree there always is anyway, because there are just some things that the recipe can never tell you — for example, that the tomatoes you're about to use are not quite as sweet as the ones you bought last week. They might be close, but the subtle nuances that change acidity or sugar levels can affect the flavour of the final dish. And for me, trying to figure out that little final ingredient that the recipe needs can be the most rewarding part of cooking. You know, like when you've just finished the sauce and you break out the spoon and do the taste test and you think, "Hmm, it's good but it needs a little …" Learning to add a touch of honey or sugar to balance excess acidity, or to add a little more salt to bring out the rest of the flavours, gives you the most amazing feeling of accomplishment.

So I suggest you ease into a recipe by reading it thoroughly so you know the process and sticking to the major ingredients. The herbs, seasonings, onions, flavouring liquids and so on can be interpreted your way, once you've trashed the training wheels.

cooking terms

Part of being able to break away from my recipes means understanding the cooking terms thoroughly. Here is a list of terms that I use over and over again in my book.

AL DENTE
The literal translation from the Italian is "to the tooth," and it means having a bit of bite or some texture. You'll usually read about cooking pasta or rice until al dente. This means you stop cooking it before it's soft and bordering on mushy.

BLANCH
This is the invaluable process of plunging vegetables (usually) into rolling boiling water just until they soften ever so slightly, and then (usually) dropping them into cold water to stop the cooking process. Blanching keeps green vegetables green and helps them retain their texture.

DEGLAZE
A one-word way to say "add a liquid such as wine or stock to the pan you just seared some food in, bring quickly to a boil and stir to scrape up all the crispy bits and pan juices for added flavour."

DREDGE

This means to lightly dip something in crumbs, flour or any other dry mixture before cooking.

GARNISH

I often list ingredients in a recipe followed by "for garnish." That just means it's not an integral part of the recipe. It just dresses up the plate or adds an accent of flavour to the final dish, like a lemon wedge or a sprinkling of chopped herbs.

MINCE

This means to chop very finely. It releases the most oils from herbs or garlic and gives you a smooth texture.

PURÉE

To mash foods in a food processor or blender or to push through a food mill until smooth. It's a process commonly used for soups and sauces and to make pastes.

REDUCE

This means simmering or boiling a sauce, stock or other liquid to evaporate some of the liquid and reduce the volume. Reducing concentrates the flavour. I usually use a wide pot so that my sauce will reduce more quickly.

ROUGHLY CHOP

I call for herbs to be roughly chopped when I want to keep a little more body to them. It also takes less time since you don't have to be too fussy about keeping things uniform. Vegetables can also be roughly chopped for stock or soup.

SAUTÉ

This is probably the most common cooking direction in my recipes. It means "to jump" in French, and it simply means to toss or stir quickly in a skillet over high heat. (By the way, it's properly pronounced "soh-tay," not "saw-tay." Both have become accepted, though.)

SEAR

To begin cooking something (usually meat or fish) in a very hot, oiled pan. This process creates a golden brown surface and helps to seal in juices.

a guide to substitutions

When I talk about experimenting with substitutions, I don't mean dismantling the entire recipe and changing absolutely everything. Nor do you *have* to change anything. But it's helpful to know what your options are.

First off, it's useful to try grouping ingredients in categories: salty, tangy or sour, sweet, spicy, floral, earthy, pungent, bitter, robust, creamy and so on.

Let's say you open up this book and you want to make Linguine with Lemon, Olive Oil and Toasted Garlic (page 73). It's your first time making the recipe, but you discover that you forgot to pick up the fresh parsley or someone fed it to the rabbit. A decision has to be made. What do you use instead? Start by looking at what the parsley's role is in the dish. Is it merely a colourful garnish, or is it carrying most of the flavour in the pasta sauce?

The recipe says 1/3 cup of parsley added at the end of the cooking. That tells you two things. First, it's a massive component of the overall flavour, and, second, it's going to maintain that fresh, bright herbal boost that parsley is known for. If you decide to just leave out the parsley, the sauce will be a tad flat, because lemon and garlic are the only other major flavour ingredients. If you decide to use some of the dried parsley flakes from the back of the cupboard, I predict the pasta will take on a much more stale, weak taste. I suggest your other option is to use another herb.

Now we're on to something. Say you rummage through the fridge and find fresh rosemary way at the back behind that last lemon. Smell is a good first test. One whiff of rosemary tells you that she's robust, earthy and intense. She's far from delicate and soft like parsley. Based on that, you can bet that rosemary will completely overwhelm your simple sauce of garlic and lemon.

Or let's say you have some leftover fresh basil in your fridge. Granted, with its sweet, peppery flavour, it will be a bit stronger than parsley, but it will deliver flavour and good balance to the lemon and garlic. Another possibility is fresh chives, which are young and delicate in flavour, much like parsley.

As a rule, I suggest you substitute herbs in the same general category — refer to my "Helpful Herb Tips" on page 30. You could use any of the soft, delicate herbs in the "delicate" category in place of parsley. Similarly, if you're looking for a rosemary substitute, pick something from the "robust" category for a closer match.

Let's take another example. Say you want to make the Thai-Spiced Chicken Drumsticks but you couldn't find fish sauce or sesame oil when you went shopping. What do you do?

Think of the primary flavour characteristic of fish sauce. Salty, right? If you look at the following list of ingredients, under "Salty" you'll see that the only other thing to substitute for fish sauce would be soy sauce (the seaweed in the list has a salty flavour but it isn't a sauce). Now for the sesame oil. You'd imagine that it's nutty tasting, so any other nut oil would work, but maybe the easiest thing to do is use an equal amount of vegetable oil and add some sesame seeds to the dish. You get the idea.

Take a look at the categories below and the ingredients that I've grouped within each. Here's your starting point for trying to use one ingredient in place of another. I've further grouped the ingredients together for similar use in a recipe. Take the "Salty" category as an example. If you don't have capers, then anchovies, caviar or clam juice would be the best substitutions, but you wouldn't want to use smoked salmon or feta cheese. (Or maybe you would, and you'd come up with your own killer recipe!)

Keep in mind that this list is meant just to give you an idea of what things taste like. The ingredients have similar tastes but they are not the same. If ingredients appear in more than one category, that means they have more than one flavour. Capers, for example, are both salty and sour.

SALTY

- soy sauce, fish sauce, seaweed
- capers, anchovies or anchovy paste, caviar or fish roe, miso, clam juice
- feta cheese, Parmigiano-Reggiano cheese
- prosciutto, smoked salmon, pancetta

SOUR/ACIDIC

- lemons, limes, blood oranges, grapefruits, vinegar, white wine, dry vermouth, pomegranate molasses
- pickles/gherkins, capers, sumac
- buttermilk, yogurt, sour cream, crème fraîche
- elderberries, blackberries, gooseberries, rhubarb, currants, cranberries, crabapples

SWEET

- basil, mint, lavender
- sugar, brown sugar, molasses, honey, maple syrup, corn syrup, barley malt
- beets, tomatoes, onions
- dates, figs, raisins, prunes
- late-harvest wine, sweet sherry, Sauternes, ice wine, brandy

BITTER

- frisée (greens), endive, radicchio, dandelion, rapini
- blood oranges, kumquats, grapefruits

SPICY/PICANTE

- arugula, watercress, basil, mint, nasturtiums
- black pepper, white pepper, long pepper, Szechuan pepper, chiles
- ginger, horseradish, mustard

CREAMY

- Brie, Camembert, soft goat cheese
- butter, cream, coconut milk

EARTHY/WOODY

- mushrooms, truffles, sage

christine's top 10 spices

In order of the most frequently used:
- freshly cracked black pepper (a given!)
- cumin seeds
- cinnamon
- coriander seeds
- fennel seeds
- saffron
- allspice
- nutmeg
- cloves
- star anise

helpful herb tips

Picking the appropriate herb for a dish can take a little practice, but if you don't experiment, you'll only be using my suggestions. Here are a few guidelines to get you started.

I put herbs into two separate categories: "robust" and "delicate." This is useful information both for substituting herbs and for knowing when to add them in the cooking process. Here's my breakdown:

ROBUST HERBS
- bay leaf, marjoram, oregano, rosemary, sage, savory, thyme

DELICATE HERBS
- basil, chervil, chives, coriander, dill, lavender, mint, parsley, tarragon

I like to cook the robust (usually twiggy) herbs, since they all develop a balanced flavour as they cook. These robust herbs also lend themselves better to drying for later use.

The delicate herbs, au contraire, need a loving, delicate hand and can often be used without cooking; they tend to lose their flavour when cooked. They can be hand torn to avoid bruising and should always be added at the end of the cooking so they retain their bright colour and peak flavour. (Adding basil to a sauce and cooking it for hours completely destroys its incredible peppery sweet fragrance and turns it grey.)

When you need to substitute, choose a herb from the same category. For example, mint and basil are much more interchangeable than mint and rosemary.

my uninhibited suggestions

Parsley, chervil and chives are good alternatives for one another as they all have a bright, fresh leafy flavour, although chervil has a slight anise or licorice flavour.

Tarragon is hard to substitute with success because of its characteristic strong licorice flavour. Chervil is similar but milder. Try using fennel seeds or anise seeds instead.

Thyme and rosemary are a great duo and work well in place of one another. I always use them with roasted potatoes, meats and chicken. Thyme is slightly more versatile as it's a tad less pushy. Thyme also works with some hearty fish, but rosemary can easily over-whelm them. Check out the Oven-Roasted Potato Wedges with Rosemary on page 119.

Basil, oregano and marjoram have a love affair with tomatoes. Do not hesitate to add any or all of these herbs to cooked tomatoes; add the oregano and marjoram at the beginning and the basil at the end. Try the Spicy Meat Sauce on page 49.

Coriander seems to be out there on its own, and you either love it or hate it. If your dish is Thai or Vietnamese, throw it in. You can use parsley, but it won't be the same; mint is another option, but it will give you a sweeter result. Try substituting equal parts of mint and parsley. Check out the Vietnamese Grilled Flank Steak on page 106.

Sage is another loner. It has a musty, earthy flavour that ends on a bitter note. It's a tough one to describe. Try using rosemary and/or thyme as a stand-in. It's great in stuffings and with onions, apples and smoked meats. It's amazing over Pumpkin Amaretti Ravioli (see page 148).

Dill is great with fish, potatoes, lamb, spinach and almost anything Greek, really. Use parsley and/or fennel tops in its place. Try the Romano Bean and Spinach Sauté on page 69.

good with ...

Beef	thyme, rosemary, parsley, mint, basil, tarragon, chives, coriander
Chicken	thyme, rosemary, parsley, mint, basil, tarragon, chives, oregano, coriander, bay leaves, sage
Fish	parsley, chives, dill, oregano, coriander, thyme, basil
Game	sage, rosemary, thyme, lavender, bay leaves, tarragon
Lamb	mint, dill, coriander, basil, oregano, rosemary, lavender, anything green
Pasta	basil, parsley, tarragon, oregano, coriander (with Asian noodles), chives
Pork	coriander, sage, thyme, rosemary
Potatoes	rosemary, thyme, parsley, chives, dill, oregano
Seafood	dill, parsley, coriander, chervil, chives

body builders

One of the best ways to enhance flavour in a dish is to build body or depth. Here are a few ingredients to start you thinking about your options and help reduce your fear factor.

My favourite body builders are:
- Dijon mustard, wine, reduced stocks, tomato paste and coconut milk

Others include:
- tomatoes, tomato purée, ketchup, hoisin sauce, BBQ sauce
- cream, butter, cheese
- sherry, vermouth, brandy, beer, port
- meat stocks, pan juices
- lime juice, lemon juice, clam juice, balsamic vinegar
- worcestershire sauce, miso

christine's favourite fearless ingredients

Here's my list of out-of-the-ordinary ingredients for creative cooking.

APPLE BUTTER

A dark and creamy reduction of pure apples; it doesn't contain any butter. It's fantastic as a low-fat source of moisture and sweetness in cakes and muffins. I also use it in marinades for pork. Apple sauce can be a substitute, but it contains much more moisture and less flavour. Available in health stores and at farmers' markets.

BARLEY MALT

This viscous dark syrup comes from sprouted barley. It's a great substitute for honey, maple syrup or molasses and is not quite as sweet. It's available mostly in health food stores.

BUFFALO MOZZARELLA

Once you have real mozzarella (in Italy it's often made with buffalo milk), you'll find it hard to go back to what we find in the supermarkets. Buffalo milk mozzarella is delicate and creamy, and it gives pizza and calzone a brilliant flavour. I go to specialty markets and cheese shops to find it.

CHIPOTLE CHILE

This dried smoked jalapeño chile should be soaked in hot water to rehydrate it before using. I use it in salsas, as a crust for chicken and meat, in mayonnaise and in soup. My sous-chef Juan is always freaking out when I don't pronounce it "chi-poh-tlay." Look for it in Latin markets and in spice stores.

CHORIZO

A spicy ground pork sausage that can be bought smoked or fresh. It's huge in Spanish and Mexican cuisines and varies immensely depending on its origin. I love using it because it adds so much depth and intensity to sauces and fillings. It's available at Spanish or specialty butchers. A spicy Italian sausage can be substituted with a similar result.

CIPOLLINI ONIONS

I love using these little Italian flat mild onions. They're similar to pearl onions but are so much more interesting visually and have a sweet, mild flavour. You can always use pearl onions in their place.

FISH SAUCE

This sauce is a staple in Vietnamese and Thai cooking and has many incarnations around the world. Its main component is salt but it's also fermented, so it has a unique flavour. It's used in stir-fries, dressings, dipping sauces and Pad Thai. It's a bit stinky, but I can't live without it.

GRANA PADANO CHEESE

This is the cousin of Parmigiano-Reggiano. The two cheeses are made in neighbouring regions with similar milk. Grana Padano is milder, since its aging time can vary from 12 to 24 months, shorter than Parmesan's.

HERBES DE PROVENCE

I've loved using this herb blend since I first went to France. The fragrance and flavour are completely different from any other and illustrate how intense a dried herb blend can be. It's hard to recreate the right balance at home, but you can try combining dried thyme, basil, marjoram, lavender, rosemary and sage for the most common mix. It's the south of France in a jar. Available at specialty shops and gourmet grocers and markets.

ISRAELI COUSCOUS

In my house this is fondly known as little white balls. It's my favourite kind of couscous. It's a pasta made of durum semolina that is rolled into a dough and then toasted. It has a chewier texture than the finer North African couscous. Look for it in Middle Eastern groceries.

JICAMA

Jicama is a crispy root vegetable that's almost a cross between a water chestnut and an apple. It's been used in Mexico for years. I prefer using it raw in a salad to add a crisp sweet bite. It should be stored in the fridge and peeled before slicing. It makes a great slaw.

LEMON GRASS

One of the most essential ingredients in Thai cooking and one of my favourite flavourings for soup, lemon grass has a tangy flavour and fragrance similar to lemon peel. It's also known as citronella, and the scent always reminds me of those mosquito candles. Thai food enthusiasts swear that you should leave the leaves in your cooking, but I find no matter how finely I chop it, it still has the texture of straw. I always strain it out or chop it more coarsely so I don't actually eat it. You can dry it and keep it in a sealed container or even freeze it wrapped in foil for a few weeks. I buy it at Asian stores and markets, although many supermarkets carry it now. Peel off the tough outer leaves, and use only the lower several inches, not the tough, grassy leaves.

LIME LEAVES

Lime leaves have a similar flavour to lemon grass and are the beautiful leaves of the kaffir lime tree from Southeast Asia, among other places. They are so fragrant in soups and sauces. They're sold fresh or dried in Asian stores. You can substitute lemon grass or grated lime zest, although neither is an exact match.

MASCARPONE CHEESE

Mascarpone is cream cheese, but it is so creamy, sweet and smooth that I have used it in all kinds of new ways. I blend it with whipping cream and lemon for a great icing for carrot cake, for example. The best mascarpone comes from Lombardy, in Italy, and you can expect to pay a good $10 for a tub. You can substitute cream cheese or sometimes ricotta, but your final product will be quite different.

MIRIN

I love using this sweet Japanese rice wine. Don't confuse it with rice wine vinegar, which is acidic. Mirin is great in dressings, sauces and soups. Look for it in Asian stores. When I can't find it, I sometimes use rice wine vinegar with a little sugar, but the acidity gives me a tangier outcome.

MISO

Miso is becoming a lot easier to find these days, but the best place to buy it — besides a Japanese grocery — is still the health food store. Everyone's surprised to know it's made of fermented soy beans; it has an intense flavour and is high in protein and vitamin B. The Japanese use it extensively in soups, sauces and marinades. You can't make miso soup without it (obviously). It's high on my list of flavour boosters to have on hand in the fridge.

MUTSU APPLES

These crisp, tart apples (also known as Crispins) are my pick for the best apple pie. They are the firmest apple in general, have a slightly tangy edge and hold their shape brilliantly when cooked.

NORI

Nori are the paper-thin sheets of seaweed that are used to wrap sushi. They have a distinctive nutty sea flavour that can add another dimension to soups and broths. If you can't find them already toasted, you can take the sheets out of their wrappers and toast them over an open flame to give them a nuttier flavour. Nori can be purchased in sushi shops and specialty Japanese stores.

PANCETTA

If I had a grain of sand for every time I used pancetta, I'd be lying on a beach right now! Pancetta is an Italian rolled bacon that is salted but not smoked. It has a firmer texture than bacon and a flavour that I can't do without. I use it in sauces, in risotto and in stuffings.

PANKO

Panko is another wonderful ingredient that was introduced to us by the Japanese. These light and fluffy bread crumbs make a great crust for cooked foods or base for tempura batter. I buy it in fish markets (where sushi-grade fish is sold), Asian markets and upscale gourmet shops. It may also say "Japanese bread crumbs" on the label.

PHYLLO

Phyllo is the Greek word for leaf or sheet and is a paper-like pastry that is used in a myriad of dishes, from sweet to savoury. It's such an amazing way to add texture to a simple recipe. I always recommend buying it at Greek stores, because they sell a ton and you can be certain it's fresh. I also suggest buying a couple of packages at a time, because you never really know how fresh it is until you open it. I have the most luck with frozen phyllo. I defrost it in the fridge for at least 8 hours to prevent cracking.

POMEGRANATE MOLASSES

Here's an unusual ingredient that has been around forever in the Middle East but is still a novelty in North America. I am addicted to it: I find it gives such a great balance of sweet and sour along with a rich crimson colour and viscosity to sauces and chutneys. It's available in Middle Eastern and Arabic stores and some specialty groceries. In ethnic stores it's also called grenadine, but don't confuse it with the cocktail grenadine. I substitute honey or lemon juice, but not regular molasses.

SAFFRON

This spice (technically an herb) has the enviable honour of being the most expensive in the world, because the threads are the stamens of crocus flowers and have to be hand picked. With saffron, a little goes a long way, though, so you need only a few threads to give a brilliant yellow colour and an intense flavour. It is always most potent in thread form versus powdered, and there is no such thing as real saffron that is cheap. Look out for imposters.

SEA SALT

Salt is such a popular topic of discussion these days, and sea salt in particular has such a distinct flavour and texture. It's made by evaporating sea water, a process that leaves all the minerals in the salt and gives it its greyish hue. It does not contain additives, so it does tend to clump, but many cooks love its natural flavour.

SUMAC

This dried berry, native to Italy and parts of the Middle East, is quickly finding its way into my recipes. It's not to be confused with the North American sumac tree, but is a bush whose berries are dried and ground. It has a pleasant tangy flavour that is used in rice, vegetable, fish and chicken dishes throughout the Middle East. Look for it in Lebanese, Middle Eastern and some specialty groceries.

SZECHUAN PEPPERCORNS

These berries are the key ingredient of Chinese five-spice powder. They come from China and look just like black peppercorns, although they're not in the same family. Their flavour is unique but difficult to describe. It reminds me of a combination of pepper, allspice and fennel. I usually find them in Asian specialty stores and spice stores. You can substitute black peppercorns, but they aren't quite the same.

TAMARI

I often suggest using good-quality soy sauce in my recipes because it has a smoother flavour with more depth and is less salty than regular supermarket brands. I always say that price is a great indicator of quality for soy sauce. Tamari is similar to soy sauce and is made in Japan. Whenever a recipe calls for soy sauce I always choose tamari. Find your favourite, but avoid the heavy, salty Chinese varieties marked by their very dark colour and inexpensive price tag. I find they make foods way too salty.

TAMARIND

I love using this sour pulp that comes from inside a date-like pod that grows on the tamarind tree. It has a very tangy flavour and a rich texture. It's used a lot in Indian and Southeast Asian cuisine; if you've had pad thai, you've had tamarind. You can buy it as a pulp with the seeds removed or in a package with seeds still intact. I find I get most flavour with the kind that still has the seeds. To remove seeds, just soak tamarind in hot water, then press it through a sieve, discarding the seeds. Asian and East Indian stores are your best bet for finding these tart pods.

VANILLA BEANS

My fridge is never without vanilla beans. They are becoming easier to find and go such a long way. Cut the bean open lengthwise and scrape out the flavourful seeds. I stick the empty pod into my sugar bowl to flavour the sugar for weeks to come. I usually suggest that 1 vanilla bean is the equivalent of 2 tsp. vanilla extract. Things never taste the same without the fresh bean, though. If you plan on using extract, avoid the kind labelled "artificial" — it's simply artificial materials that are chemically treated, and it has little resemblance to "pure vanilla extract." Tahitian beans are plump and soft, although most people argue that their flavour is not as intense as that of the thinner Madagascar variety. Good beans also come from Mexico.

stripped
down

To get your senses stimulated and begin your journey into being fearless in the kitchen in this chapter I feature recipes that are basic but allow for many variations and substitutions. These recipes focus on basic techniques rather than on specific ingredients precise quantities. Take what you learned in chapter and practise your hand at substitutions. Many of the recipes are also basics that you can build a dish around like the Any Lettuce Dressing. You can create your own favourite salad with this everyday dressing that's loaded with flavour.

homemade chicken stock

I always start my stock with plenty of chicken bones — carcasses, back bones, ribs, wings and feet. They may look ugly, but they are major flavour boosters.

For more depth of flavour in my stock, I roast the bones first, then follow the regular procedure. This gives me a richer, sweeter, darker stock that is great for sauces, soups and pasta dishes. Check out the Pantry Pasta recipe on page 74. It uses roasted chicken stock.

If you don't have a pot big enough to hold the chicken bones and 18 cups of water, relax — just make half the recipe.

about 4 lb. (2 kg) raw chicken bones (backs, feet, ribs, wings, necks)
2 large onions, chopped
2 large carrots, chopped
2 stalks celery, chopped
1 leek, cleaned well and chopped
bouquet garni (made with a few sprigs each fresh thyme and rosemary,
    8 to 10 whole peppercorns, 1 or 2 whole cloves and 2 or 3 bay leaves)*
about 18 cups (4.5 L) cold water

Rinse chicken bones well under cold water. Transfer to an 8-quart (8 L) stockpot. Add the onions, carrots, celery, leek and the bouquet garni. Add enough cold water to cover and bring to a boil over high heat. As the water comes to a boil, skim off the scum that floats on top.

When the water comes to a boil, reduce heat to low and simmer stock very gently, uncovered, for at least 2 hours or up to 5 hours if you want a more concentrated flavour. The liquid should barely bubble; if the stock boils it will be cloudy. And don't stir it or push down on the bones — that will make it cloudy too.

Strain the stock through a fine sieve and cool. Store in airtight containers in the freezer until ready to use. Skim off the fat from the top of the stock before using.

MAKES ABOUT 16 CUPS (4 L), BUT YIELD DEPENDS ON HOW LONG YOU SIMMER THE STOCK

✱ To make a bouquet garni, tie the herbs and spices in a square of cheesecloth. In this case, though, since you're going to strain the stock, you could just throw the flavourings straight into the pot.

my homemade chicken soup

I think if I were to ask my mom for a good recipe for chicken soup, she'd say, "What recipe? You don't need a recipe. Make it with some love and some good chicken bones — and then you've got a good soup." A comforting homemade chicken soup starts with the stock. It's all about getting the flavour out of the bones. Whether you add veggies, rice or anything your heart desires to the soup, it absolutely has to start with a good stock.

2 tbsp. butter (25 mL)

1 onion, chopped

2 carrots, chopped

1 stalk celery, chopped

4 skinless chicken thighs

8 cups chicken stock (2 L)

2 sprigs fresh thyme

1 bay leaf

1/2 cup rice (125 mL)

salt and pepper to taste

In a large saucepan, melt butter over medium heat. Sauté onion, carrots and celery for 3 to 5 minutes, or until soft. Add chicken thighs, stock, thyme and bay leaf. Bring to a boil and reduce heat to low. Simmer, uncovered, for 30 to 35 minutes, or until chicken is cooked through and tender.

Remove chicken thighs from the soup and take meat off the bones. Return the meat to the soup; add rice and season with salt and pepper. Simmer until rice is tender, 12 to 15 minutes. Discard bay leaf before serving.

SERVES 8

other comforting soups to try

Chicken Lemon Soup (Avgolemono) (page 63)

Miso Noodle Soup (page 62)

buttermilk biscuits

Here is a rare case where I strongly recommend using the amounts given in the recipe so that the chemical structure of the biscuit is not affected. We're now in the realm of baking, and a formula is critical. But that doesn't mean you can't add your favourite flavourings to make these biscuits your own. I make these both sweet and savoury, and either way they are tender and crisp with a sweet, buttery finish.

2 1/4 cups all-purpose flour (550 mL)

1 1/2 tsp. baking powder (7 mL)

1/2 tsp. baking soda (2 mL)

1/4 tsp. salt (1 mL)

1/3 cup very cold butter (75 mL), cut into small pieces

3/4 cup buttermilk (175 mL)

1 egg, whisked with 1 tbsp. (15 mL) water

In a food processor, combine the flour, baking powder, baking soda and salt. Pulse until blended. Add the cold butter and pulse until mixture resembles coarse meal. Transfer to a bowl and stir in milk until mixture just comes together. Do not overmix or the biscuits will be tough.

Turn onto a lightly floured surface and gently knead a few times until dough just holds together. Again, don't overwork the dough or the biscuits will be tough. Wrap dough in plastic wrap or parchment paper and chill for 30 minutes.

Preheat oven to 375°F. Line a 9- by 12-inch baking sheet with parchment paper, or brush baking sheet with butter.

On a lightly floured surface, roll out dough to 1/2-inch (1 cm) thickness. Using a 2 1/4-inch (5.5 cm) round cookie cutter, cut 12 rounds and place them on the baking sheet. Gather the scraps together and you can probably make 2 more biscuits (waste not, want not!). Brush biscuits with eggwash. Bake until golden and lightly browned, 18 to 20 minutes.

MAKES ABOUT 12 BISCUITS (PLUS 2 COOK'S TREATS)

variations

Dinner Biscuits: Add a finely diced small firm apple and some shredded sharp cheese. A great dinner accompaniment, especially with baked ham.

Quick Shortcakes: Add a spoonful of poppy seeds, the grated zest of a citrus fruit and a touch of sugar. These are easy shortcakes for strawberries and cream.

Italian Biscuits: Replace 1/4 cup of the flour with semolina. Add chopped fresh thyme and a pinch of cracked black pepper. Voila, a savoury, crunchy biscuit with a bit of a kick.

bistro frites

Frites, fries, chips — whatever you want to call them, they are awesome. I don't make these every day, but they sure beat those greasy, battered dipped things that you get in fast-food places. Frying the potatoes twice ensures that you'll get crispy fries. Sometimes I fry some extra potatoes during the first frying, let them drain and cool completely, then spread them out on a baking sheet and freeze them. I store the fries in freezer bags so I have quick easy fries that I can fry straight from the freezer.

6 large Yukon Gold or baking potatoes
4 cups vegetable oil (1 L)
salt and freshly cracked black pepper to taste

Peel potatoes and cut into 1/4-inch-thick (5 mm) sticks. Soak in water for at least 2 hours. Drain the potatoes and dry them very well.

In a deep saucepan, heat the oil until it reaches 330°F. Fry the potatoes in small batches for about 3 minutes, or until just cooked through but not browned. Drain on paper towels and cool to room temperature.

Heat the oil to 375°F. Fry the potatoes again for 1 to 2 minutes, or until golden brown and crispy. Drain on paper towels. Season the frites immediately with salt and pepper.

SERVES 4

variation
Frites with a Belgian Makeover: Add a Belgian twist to your frites and serve them with a creamy dipping sauce. Just stir some minced garlic, lemon juice and a pinch of cayenne into mayonnaise. Dip away.

any lettuce dressing

I'm a salad freak, but if the dressing doesn't cut it, I'm moving on to the next course. Salad dressing is the perfect starting point to having fun and being fearless with a recipe. It's not a big production, it's easy to adjust, and there are tons of variations. I never measure when I make a dressing. I just check the taste by dipping a leaf of the greens I'm using in the salad.

You may find my dressings mouth-puckeringly tangy. The old cooking-school rule of 3 parts oil to 1 part acid doesn't work for me. Bring on the tang! (But if you find the taste too tangy, just add a bit more oil and a touch more honey.)

1 shallot, minced
1/4 cup apple cider vinegar (60 mL)
1/4 cup buttermilk (60 mL)
1/4 cup safflower oil (60 mL)
1 tsp. honey (5 mL)
1 tsp. Dijon mustard (5 mL)
grated zest and juice of 1/2 lemon
salt and cracked black pepper to taste

In a bowl, combine all ingredients and whisk well (or shake in a jar). Toss any amount of dressing you like with your favourite greens (some people like their salad lightly covered and some like it dripping). Serve immediately.

MAKES 1 CUP (250 ML), ENOUGH FOR A SALAD SERVING 6 TO 8

variations

For an even tangier bite: Instead of apple cider vinegar, use sherry vinegar, white wine or red wine vinegar and balance with a touch more honey.

For a simple Italian twist: Omit the buttermilk. Instead of apple cider vinegar, use balsamic vinegar. Instead of safflower oil, use extra virgin olive oil.

compound butters

I'm including these recipes because they top the chef's list for instant flavour. Compound butter is just a culinary term for pumped-up flavoured butter. It can be sweet or savoury. The best part is you can make it ahead and jam it in the freezer until you have the perfect canvas. Spread the Cinnamon Sugar Butter on toast or pancakes for a sweet start to your morning. Or make a savoury variation: one day it's melting over fresh fish, the next it's kissing grilled meat, and another day it's oozing all over your pasta. Butter has almost every other ingredient begging to be in the same bowl. I try to pick an appropriate mate for butter's sweet, rich and creamy flavour — to compound great taste!

CINNAMON SUGAR BUTTER

1/2 lb. unsalted butter (250 g), cut into small pieces, at room temperature

1/2 vanilla bean, scraped, or 1 tsp. vanilla (2 mL)

2 tbsp. dark brown sugar (25 mL)

1/2 tsp. cinnamon (2 mL)

In a stand mixer with paddle attachment or in a bowl with an electric beater, whip butter on medium speed for about 2 minutes, or until it is light and fluffy. Occasionally scrape down sides so butter is evenly whipped. Add the vanilla, sugar and cinnamon. Beat for 3 to 4 minutes, or until mixture is smooth and fluffy. On a large rectangle of plastic wrap, spread compound butter in a log shape. Roll up into a log and twist the ends of plastic tightly to seal. Refrigerate or freeze until ready to use.

MAKES ABOUT 1/2 LB. (250 G)

variations

Mediterranean Burst: To 1/2 lb. whipped butter, add a few tablespoons chopped fresh parsley, some capers, the grated zest of 1 lemon and a minced clove of garlic. Serve over any grilled fish or seafood.

Asian Tang: To 1/2 lb. whipped butter, add the grated zest of 1 lime and a tablespoon each of sesame seeds and finely minced lemon grass. Serve over chicken or seafood.

Mexican Spice: To 1/2 lb. whipped butter, add a small chipotle chile that has been soaked and finely diced and a couple of tablespoons chopped fresh coriander. Serve with chicken, beef or lamb.

spiced salts

There is such a buzz about salt these days, and I'm the first in line to sing the praises of fleur de sel. I think it's great that so many different salts are available now. Flavouring your own salt is such a cool — and easy — way to put your own signature on a dish and dazzle family and friends at the table. For maximum flavour, use within a few weeks, because the flavour will begin to dissipate. Spices, herbs and other flavouring agents are all fair game so long as you don't add anything wet. I prefer citrus zests, bold spices and of course garlic. I also choose robust herbs such as thyme and rosemary rather than delicate leafy herbs such as basil.

HERBED SALT

2 sprigs fresh rosemary

2 sprigs fresh thyme

2 cloves garlic, cut in half lengthwise

1 bay leaf

1 cup coarse sea salt (250 mL)

Preheat oven to 375°F.

Spread herb sprigs, garlic and bay leaf on a baking sheet. Cover with the salt. Bake for 20 minutes. Let cool. Discard garlic and bay leaf. Remove the leaves of the herbs and stir into the salt. Store salt in an airtight container for up to 3 weeks.

MAKES 1 CUP (250 ML)

variation

Moroccan Spiced Salt: To 1 cup coarse sea salt, add a broken whole cinnamon stick, a few whole allspice berries, several coriander seeds and a few slices of fresh ginger. Bake as described for Herbed Salt. If you want the intensity of the spices in the salt, coarsely grind the baked salt mixture with the whole spices in a mortar and pestle or small coffee grinder. If you want only a subtle flavour of the spices, remove them.

bsteeya (moroccan chicken pie), p. 144

spanish rice with sherry sautéed shrimp, p. 97

pumpkin amaretti ravioli, p. 148

spicy meat sauce

Just about every country on the planet has a version of meat sauce, from bolognese to chili to goulash. The Mediterranean seems to feature the most variations, and in my Spicy Meat Sauce, I use the Italian philosophy of simplicity with the greatest attention to the quality of the ingredients. The Italian philosophy seems to work, because I don't think I've ever had an average meat sauce in Italy. I prefer to ask my butcher to grind the beef rather than buying it already packaged. I also use good-quality plum tomatoes, luscious extra virgin olive oil and an accent of cayenne or a chile. I find myself using bread to mop up every last drop of sauce on my plate!

3 tbsp. extra virgin olive oil (45 mL)	several sprigs fresh thyme
2 onions, finely chopped	dried oregano to taste
1 1/2 lb. lean ground beef (750 g)	couple bay leaves
1 small spicy Italian sausage, casing removed	cayenne or fresh chile to taste
2 cloves garlic, chopped	1 can (28 oz./796 mL) plum tomatoes with juice, chopped
2 small carrots, finely diced	salt and freshly cracked black pepper to taste

In a large skillet, heat oil over medium-high heat. Add the onions and sauté 3 to 4 minutes, or until soft. Add the beef and sausage; cook, stirring frequently, for 5 to 7 minutes, or until meat is nicely browned. Add the garlic and carrots; sauté for 3 minutes just to soften.

Add thyme, oregano, bay leaves, cayenne, tomatoes, salt and pepper. Bring to a boil, reduce heat to low and simmer, covered, for about 1 hour, or until sauce is thickened and flavour has developed to your liking. The longer you cook it, the more intense the meat sauce gets. Adjust seasoning. Discard thyme sprigs and bay leaves before serving.

MAKES ABOUT 6 CUPS (1.5 L)

variations

North African Aromatic: Replace half the beef with ground lamb, add several threads of saffron and a pinch each of cinnamon and ground cloves. Throw in a handful of raisins for that special Moroccan sweet kick. Use mint and parsley in place of the basil and thyme.

Cajun: Add as many fresh chiles as you can take, some pan-fried okra and diced potatoes, and you have an instant Louisiana chili.

breakfast substitute fruit smoothie

The smoothie is one of my all-time faves for a quick, healthful breakfast. You honestly don't need a recipe: just blend some juice with something sweet (like a banana), something a little tart (like blackberries) and something real creamy (like yogurt). If you don't like any seeds or extra fibre, strain the smoothie through a sieve before serving.

1 heaping cup blackberries (300 mL)

1 cup peach nectar (250 mL)

1 small container plain yogurt (about 6 oz./175 mL)

1 banana

1 1/2 cups orange juice (375 mL)

Combine all ingredients in a blender and pulse until smooth.

SERVES 4

variations

Cranberry Smoothie: Use cranberries instead of blackberries and use apple juice instead of peach nectar.

Mango and Raspberry Smoothie: Use raspberries instead of blackberries and use mango nectar instead of peach nectar.

Kiwi Boost: Add kiwis to any smoothie for vitamin C and a crunchy texture.

Killer Shake: Turn the smoothie into a shake by replacing the yogurt with vanilla ice cream and adding some crushed ice.

the perfect omelette

Ah, the perfect omelette. How can the simple combination of eggs and some seasoning just fried in a pan have so many permutations? It's too wet, too dry, too mushy or too dark. Oy. The perfect omelette is all about how you make it and not necessarily what goes in it. You definitely have to have the technique down. It takes a bit of practice, but once you've done it a few times, you'll get the hang of it and be able to show off. It also helps to have a well-seasoned omelette pan (see page 53), one with high sides so you don't end up with your omelette all over the stovetop. Three eggs in an 8-inch (20 cm) omelette pan seems to be the magic combination.

3 large eggs

1 tbsp. water (15 mL)

1 tbsp. chopped fresh chives or parsley (15 mL)

salt and freshly cracked black pepper to taste

1 1/2 tbsp. butter or olive oil (20 mL)

Combine eggs, water, chives, salt and pepper in a small bowl. Whisk together with a fork until blended.

Heat butter in an 8-inch (20 cm) omelette pan over high heat until foam subsides. Pour egg mixture into pan and swirl the pan in a circular motion until eggs are just set on top and golden but not brown on the bottom, about 1 minute. Sprinkle any kind of filling you like on top of the omelette. Using a spatula, fold one third of the omelette over to the centre of the pan. Slide the omelette out of the pan onto a plate and fold over remaining third.

SERVES 1

variations

Smooth and Creamy Omelette: Just before folding the omelette, sprinkle with crumbled soft goat cheese.

Hot and Spicy Omelette: For my version of Huevos Rancheros, just before folding the omelette, sprinkle with a touch of chunky spicy salsa, chopped fresh parsley and shredded manchego cheese.

Sharp and Salty Omelette: Just before folding the omelette, add crispy fried pancetta, chopped black Italian olives and grated asiago cheese.

crêpes

The crêpe is such a great dish to master because it's waaay easy and so versatile — it can be sweet or savoury, a first course, main course or dessert. I always make extra crêpes and freeze them in stacks, ready for drop-in guests. I recommend using a shallow crêpe pan that has been seasoned (see note below) — you'll find it makes cooking the crêpes much faster and easier.

To make dessert crêpes, just add a sprinkle of sugar to the batter.

3 eggs
1 1/4 cups milk (300 mL)
pinch salt
1/2 cup all-purpose flour (125 mL)
2 tbsp. melted butter (25 mL)

In a medium bowl, gently whisk the eggs with 1 cup (250 mL) of the milk and the salt. Sift flour over the egg mixture. Continue to gently whisk the batter until smooth. The batter should be a little thicker than whipping cream. If the batter is too thick, add the remaining 1/4 cup (50 mL) of milk. Add the melted butter and stir. Cover the batter with plastic wrap and let it rest for 30 minutes.

Heat a seasoned* 7-inch (18 cm) crêpe pan over medium-high heat. When the pan is hot, lightly brush with butter or oil. Pour 3 tbsp. (45 mL) of batter into the centre of the pan and swirl the pan so the batter spreads to make a thin pancake. Cook about 1 minute. When the crêpe is lightly golden on the bottom and the top starts to bubble, flip it over and cook another 30 seconds, or until lightly golden. Transfer the crêpe to a plate. Repeat with the rest of the batter, stacking the cooked crêpes.

If you're not using the crêpes immediately, tightly wrap the stack in plastic wrap and refrigerate for up to 3 days, or freeze in an airtight container.

MAKES 16 CRÊPES

variations

Oriental Spice Crêpes: Add a sprinkle of chopped fresh coriander and a handful of sesame seeds to the crêpe batter. Stuff the crêpes with thinly sliced cooked salmon. Drizzle with a mix of soy sauce, a pinch of brown sugar and a squeeze of lime juice.

Dark and Sweet Crêpes: Stuff dessert crêpes with rum-flavoured bananas. Just sauté some bananas in butter with a sprinkle of brown sugar and a splash of rum. Bananas should be soft but not mushy. Roll up and drizzle with chocolate sauce (combine 1 part melted bittersweet chocolate with 1 part hot cream and a dash of liqueur).

Fall Crêpes Canadiana: Stuff dessert crêpes with apple slices sautéed with maple syrup, allspice and brandy. Top with caramel sauce or vanilla ice cream.

✳ To season a crêpe or omelette pan: The more you use your pan, the less often crêpes or omelettes will stick. Wipe the inside of the crêpe pan with a generous amount of vegetable oil. Bake at 325°F for about an hour; wipe with more oil if the pan looks dry. For quick tune-ups, add enough oil to cover bottom of pan and heat the pan over high heat until smoking. Remove from heat and add some rock salt. With a heavy cloth, scour pan with salt to polish. Rub dry.

on the **fly**

The recipes in this chapter are quickies that yo
can make on the fly. I've included recipes from
all over the culinary map, with influences
from Asia to the Mediterranean to North America.
They include starters, quick mains and eve
a speedy dessert, Baked Pear with Roquefort and Port.
There are also a good number of side dishe
to accompany your lonely piece of chicken or fish.
Although these dishes are quick and not too fuss
they are still innovative and
will introduce you to some of
my favourite new ingredients

red pepper and feta spread (kopanisti)

This appetizer spread is great for both casual gatherings and quick weeknight I'm-hungry-right-now dinners. It's so easy to whip up. The sweet pepper balances the salty feta. Don't cut corners on the quality of your feta — it's the biggest part of the flavour.

2 red peppers, roasted, peeled and seeded
1/2 lb. good-quality feta (250 g), crumbled
1 small red chile, finely chopped, or red pepper flakes to taste
1/4 cup extra virgin olive oil (60 mL)

In a food processor, purée the roasted peppers. Add the feta and pulse a few times. Add the chile and pulse until just mixed. Transfer to a bowl. Stir in olive oil until blended. Serve with grilled pita or bread.

SERVES 10 TO 12

saffron-baked jumbo shrimp

Loaded with garlic and a good hit of fresh parsley, these shrimp are a great appetizer. You can also turn them into a simple topping for pasta or rice.

1 lb. large shrimp (about 18) (500 g), peeled, deveined, tails left on
2 or 3 cloves garlic, minced
several threads saffron
1/2 cup chopped fresh parsley (125 mL)
1/4 cup extra virgin olive oil (60 mL)
1/2 tsp. paprika (2 mL)
coarsely ground salt and pepper to taste
juice of 1 lemon

Preheat oven to 400°F.

In a large bowl, toss together the shrimp, garlic, saffron, parsley, oil, paprika, salt and pepper to coat shrimp well.

Spread shrimp in one layer on a large baking sheet. Bake for 4 to 6 minutes, or until shrimp are curled, pink and just firm. Sprinkle with lemon juice and serve at once.

SERVES 6 AS APPETIZER

smoked trout mousse

If you start making this mousse right now, by the time someone has read the directions to you, it's just about made. I have made this mousse for cocktail parties and cooking classes, and people go rangy for it. It also got me hooked on smoked trout, which has a firmer texture and sweeter flavour than smoked salmon. If you're feeling adventurous and want to smoke your own, see page 155.

about 9 oz. smoked trout (300 g)
1 cup mascarpone (250 mL)
1/3 cup whipping (35%) cream (75 mL)
juice of 1/2 lemon
2 tbsp. chopped fresh dill (25 mL)
chopped fresh chives to taste
freshly cracked black pepper
2 tbsp. capers (25 mL), for garnish

In a food processor, pulse the trout until just blended. Add the mascarpone and cream; pulse until just smooth. Transfer mixture to a bowl and stir in lemon juice, dill, chives and pepper. Cover and chill until ready to serve. Serve with crackers, grilled pita, toasts or cooked potato wedges. Top with capers.

MAKES 2 CUPS (500 ML)

seared tuna with lemon and caper dressing

Once you've made this appetizer a few times, you probably won't need a recipe. Simply rub the tuna with some fresh herbs and pop it on the grill. The tuna needs a strong dressing to make it sing, and this one, an Italian inspiration of olive oil, garlic and lots of lemon, makes the tuna sing arias. I serve the tuna over peppery arugula or escarole to give great contrast with every bite.

For best results, ask your fishmonger for sushi-grade fish, which can be eaten raw. That way, you can serve it very rare.

1/2 lb. sushi-grade tuna (250 g)

salt and cracked black pepper

2 tbsp. chopped fresh parsley (25 mL)

1 tbsp. chopped fresh coriander (15 mL)

2 tbsp. olive oil (25 mL)

1 bunch arugula

VINAIGRETTE

2 cloves garlic, minced

1 tsp. capers (5 mL)

1 tsp. Dijon mustard (5 mL)

1 small anchovy, minced (I say don't leave it out)

grated zest and juice of 1 lemon

1/4 cup extra virgin olive oil (60 mL)

salt and fresh cracked black pepper to taste

Season tuna with salt and pepper and sprinkle with parsley and coriander. In a large skillet over high heat, heat the oil. Sear tuna for about 2 minutes per side per 1 inch (2.5 cm) of thickness. Tuna should still be pink in the middle. Remove from pan and cool slightly. Slice thinly.

Combine ingredients for dressing and whisk in a bowl (or shake in a jar). Arrange tuna slices over greens and drizzle with dressing.

SERVES 4

miso noodle soup

I dreamt this recipe up one day as I was trying to come up with chicken soup options that are quick. Whisking in miso is a quick way to add an earthy flavour and complexity to an otherwise very clean tasting soup. Any kind of noodles or vegetables can be used in this speedy soup.

1 stalk lemon grass, white part only

1 large onion, chopped

1-inch piece ginger (2.5 cm), peeled and grated

2 tbsp. vegetable oil (25 mL)

8 cups chicken stock (2 L) (see page 42)

1 tbsp. soy sauce (15 mL)

2 oz. flat rice noodles (60 g), broken into pieces

3 tbsp. mild miso paste (45 mL)

2 green onions, thinly sliced

salt and pepper to taste

1 sheet nori, ripped into bite-sized pieces, for garnish

Slice the lemon grass across the grain but do not cut all the way through. (It will be easier to remove the lemon grass if it stays in one piece.) In a medium saucepan, sauté the onion and ginger in oil for 4 to 5 minutes, or until soft. Stir in the lemon grass, stock and soy sauce. Bring to a boil over high heat. Reduce heat to low and simmer, uncovered, for 20 minutes, or until the soup has reduced by a quarter.

Increase the heat to high. Stir in the noodles and boil until just tender, 3 to 4 minutes. Add the miso and remove from heat. Whisk until miso is dissolved. Add the green onions. Season with salt and pepper and discard the lemon grass. Serve soup garnished with pieces of nori.

SERVES 4 TO 6

chicken lemon soup (avgolemono)

Don't even ask me to pronounce this one in Greek. All you need to know is it's the most amazing soup there is. My brother will travel miles to have a bowlful. If you have chicken stock in your freezer or pantry, this soup can be on the table in less than 15 minutes. You can substitute rice for the orzo, but I like it better with orzo.

8 cups chicken stock (2 L) (see page 42)
3/4 cup orzo or rice (175 mL)
2 eggs
juice of 1 lemon
salt and pepper to taste

In a medium saucepan, bring stock to a boil. Stir in the orzo and simmer, uncovered, until pasta is cooked, about 10 minutes.

In a medium bowl, whisk together eggs and lemon juice until frothy. Vigorously whisk about 1 cup of the hot stock into the egg mixture. Whisk this mixture back into the hot soup and immediately remove from heat. Season with salt and pepper and serve immediately.

SERVES 4 TO 6

watercress, jicama and walnut salad

Jicama is a root vegetable that tastes like a combination of an apple and a potato and is awesome in salads for crunchy texture as well as for flavour. I put this salad in the quickie category because I often just grill a piece of chicken and ta-da ... dinner is on the table!

1 small bunch watercress, tough stems removed

several handfuls of mixed leafy green lettuce, torn into bite-sized pieces

1/2 jicama, cut into julienne strips*

1/4 cup walnut halves (60 mL)

DRESSING

1 shallot, minced

3 tbsp. sherry vinegar (45 mL)

3 tbsp. vegetable oil (45 mL)

2 tbsp. toasted peanut oil (25 mL)

1 tsp. Dijon mustard (5 mL)

1 tsp. honey (5 mL)

salt and freshly cracked black pepper to taste

Wash greens well and dry in a salad spinner or in a cloth. In a large bowl, toss greens with jicama.

Combine dressing ingredients and whisk in a bowl (or shake in a jar) until smooth. Adjust seasoning. Toss salad with half the dressing. If salad seems too dry, add more dressing. Sprinkle with walnuts. Serve remaining dressing at the table.

SERVES 4 TO 6

✳ If you can't find jicama, just use a crisp apple in its place.

chickpea, black olive and tomato salad

This salad is honestly as easy as opening a can of chickpeas and tossing in a few tomatoes. It's a variation of a Greek village salad, with some North African accents. It would be awesome with a side of grilled fish, chicken or any meat.

1 can (19 oz./540 mL) chickpeas, drained and rinsed

2 large field tomatoes, each cut into 8 wedges

1 small red onion, thinly sliced

1 clove garlic, minced

juice of 1/2 lemon

1/3 cup black olives (75 mL)

1/3 cup extra virgin olive oil (75 mL)

1/4 cup chopped fresh mint (60 mL)

1/4 cup chopped fresh parsley (60 mL)

2 tbsp. red wine vinegar (25 mL)

dried oregano to taste

1/2 tsp. ground sumac (2 mL) (optional)

salt and freshly cracked black pepper to taste

Combine all ingredients in a large bowl and toss well.

SERVES 4

israeli couscous with sweet potato

Israeli couscous is one of my all-time favourite starches. Different from North African couscous, Israeli couscous looks like pearls and has a chewier texture. The best way to add flavour to these little white balls is with sumac, which gives a pleasant tanginess. I've got to admit, I really love tang!

3 tbsp. olive oil (45 mL)

2 shallots, chopped

1 small sweet potato, peeled and diced

1/2 tsp. ground sumac (2 mL)

2 cups Israeli couscous (500 mL)

3 cups chicken or vegetable stock (750 mL)

salt and freshly cracked black pepper to taste

Heat oil in a medium saucepan over medium heat. Cook shallots until soft but not browned, about 4 minutes. Add sweet potato, sumac and couscous; cook, stirring, until couscous starts to toast, about 2 minutes. Add stock, salt and pepper. Bring to a boil. Cover and reduce heat to low. Cook the couscous for 10 to 12 minutes, or until all the liquid is absorbed and the couscous is al dente. Remove from the heat. Let stand, covered, for 5 minutes. Fluff with a fork before serving.

SERVES 4 TO 6

roasted potatoes, cipollini and herbes de provence

I was getting tired of just plain roasted potatoes, and this was my way of perking them up. Adding a handful of black olives, loads of herbes de Provence and some baby Italian onions makes the potatoes dance with any roasted meat, bird or fish. This dish is the perfect balance of salty, fragrant and sweet — and it's so easy. You can use pearl onions or shallots in place of the cipollini, but they are so cute and adorable and packed with good taste.

4 large red potatoes, scrubbed, cut in quarters

12 cipollini, peeled

3 tbsp. extra virgin olive oil (45 mL)

1 tbsp. herbes de Provence (15 mL)

salt and freshly cracked black pepper to taste

1/4 cup pitted black olives (preferably niçoise) (60 mL), slivered

Preheat oven to 375°F.

In a large roasting pan, toss together potatoes, cipollini, oil, herbes de Provence, salt and pepper. Roast for 15 minutes. Sprinkle on the olives. Roast, stirring once in a while to prevent scorching, a further 30 minutes, or until potatoes are tender and onions are soft and golden.

SERVES 4

roasted butternut squash with pine nuts and honey

This is a great starchy side to make from fall right into winter, and it takes a total of 30 minutes to prepare. The squash turns a beautiful golden brown with the addition of the soy and honey.

1/2 butternut squash, peeled and cut into 1-inch (2.5 cm) cubes

2 tbsp. honey (25 mL)

1 tbsp. good-quality soy sauce (15 mL)

1 tbsp. vegetable oil (15 mL)

dash sesame oil

pinch ground allspice

cracked black pepper to taste

1/3 cup pine nuts (75 mL)

Preheat oven to 375°F.

In a large bowl combine squash, honey, soy sauce, vegetable oil, sesame oil, allspice and pepper. Toss well to coat evenly.

Spread squash in a single layer on a baking sheet or small roasting pan. Roast, stirring several times to prevent scorching, for 15 to 20 minutes, or until squash is just tender. Add the pine nuts and roast for a further 3 minutes, or until pine nuts are just golden. Adjust seasoning and serve immediately.

SERVES 4

romano bean and spinach sauté

This quick side dish could be called Any Kind of Bean Under the Sun and Spinach Sauté. I wanted something a little more inventive than plain beans, so I just added some spinach, yellow peppers and a sprinkle of freshly chopped dill. Voila — a bean makeover! See — being fearless isn't so hard.

3 tbsp. olive oil (45 mL)

2 large shallots, chopped

2 cloves garlic, finely chopped

1 yellow pepper, diced

1 can (14 oz./398 mL) romano beans, drained and rinsed*

1 small bunch spinach, washed well, tough stems removed

2 tbsp. chopped fresh dill (25 mL)

several fresh chives, chopped

salt and pepper to taste

pinch grated nutmeg

Heat oil in a large skillet over medium-high heat. Sauté the shallots for 2 minutes, or until soft. Add the garlic; sauté for 1 minute, or until soft. Add the yellow pepper and sauté for 3 minutes. Add beans, spinach, dill, chives, salt, pepper and nutmeg. Toss just to warm through. Adjust seasoning.

SERVES 4

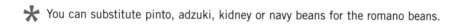 You can substitute pinto, adzuki, kidney or navy beans for the romano beans.

rapini with toasted almonds and sliced garlic

Rapini, a.k.a. broccoli rabe, is probably my favourite vegetable. I can't seem to live without it. It's also a snap to whip up in no time. The almonds give it a bit more crunch and a toasty contrast to its bitter edge.

1 bunch rapini

3 tbsp. extra virgin olive oil (45 mL)

1/3 cup toasted almonds, skin on (75 mL), coarsely chopped

1 clove garlic, thinly sliced

salt and freshly cracked black pepper to taste

lemon wedges, for garnish

Wash rapini well and trim thick stems about 2 inches (5 cm) from the bottom. Cook rapini in plenty of boiling salted water for 5 to 6 minutes, or until just tender but still firm. Drain well and transfer to a serving bowl.

Heat oil in a medium skillet over medium heat. Add the almonds; toss for 2 to 3 minutes, or until just golden. Add the garlic; toss for 2 more minutes, or until garlic is just turning golden. Immediately remove from heat and toss in reserved rapini. Season with salt and pepper. Serve immediately with lemon wedges on the side.

SERVES 4

peas and prosciutto

This simply delicious recipe once again proves that simplicity rules in the kitchen. Who knew that peas and salted ham could taste so good together?

2 cups fresh or frozen green peas (500 mL)

3 tbsp. butter (45 mL)

3 shallots or 1 onion, finely chopped

2 oz. thinly sliced prosciutto (60 g), cut in thin strips

salt and cracked black pepper to taste

freshly grated nutmeg to taste (optional)

Blanch peas in boiling water for 2 minutes. Drain and reserve.

In a medium skillet, melt the butter over medium-high heat. Sauté the shallots for 3 to 4 minutes, or until soft. Add the prosciutto and cook, tossing, until just golden, about 2 minutes. Add the peas, salt, pepper and nutmeg. Toss to warm through. Serve immediately.

SERVES 4

orzo with grilled baby eggplant and toasted pine nuts

There's always so much confusion about orzo. This rice-shaped pasta is huge in Greece, and I can't go more than a couple of weeks without it. It's so quick to cook and so versatile, too. In this dish, I happen to love grilled eggplant (especially the baby varieties, which are less bitter than the common large eggplant), but you can add just about any grilled vegetable to this canvas.

1 baby eggplant

4 tbsp. extra virgin olive oil (60 mL)

1 red pepper, cut into quarters

1 small onion, diced

1 clove garlic, minced

grated zest of 1/2 lemon

1/3 cup toasted pine nuts (75 mL)

1 small tomato, diced

1/4 cup chopped fresh mint (60 mL)

1/4 cup chopped fresh basil (60 mL)

1 lb. orzo (500 g)

1/4 cup grated Parmigiano-Reggiano (60 mL)

salt and freshly cracked black pepper to taste

Preheat grill to high.

Thinly slice the eggplant and brush both sides with half the oil. Cut red pepper into quarters. Grill eggplant and pepper, turning occasionally, until golden and soft. Remove from grill, dice and transfer to a medium bowl.

In a medium skillet, heat the remaining olive oil over medium-high heat. Sauté onion until soft, about 4 minutes. Add garlic, lemon zest and pine nuts. Sauté a minute longer just to develop flavour. Add to grilled veggies. Add tomato, mint and basil; toss together.

Cook the orzo in a pot of boiling salted water until al dente, 7 to 9 minutes. Drain well and add to vegetable mixture. Add cheese and toss together well. Season with salt and pepper and serve.

SERVES 4 TO 6

linguine with lemon, olive oil and toasted garlic

This to-die-for pasta dish comes together in the time it takes to boil the pasta. Better still, you probably have every single ingredient in your kitchen to make it right now. I particularly go crazy over the way lemon juice and parsley add a fresh tang to the toasted garlic.

1 lb. linguine (500 g)

3 cloves garlic, thinly sliced

1/4 cup extra virgin olive oil (60 mL)

grated zest and juice of 1 lemon

1/3 cup chopped fresh parsley (75 mL)

1/3 cup freshly grated Parmigiano-Reggiano (75 mL) or to taste

salt and freshly cracked black pepper to taste

Cook linguine in a large pot of boiling salted water until al dente, 9 to 11 minutes. Drain well and return to pot.

Meanwhile, in a skillet over low heat, cook garlic in olive oil for 3 to 4 minutes, or until just golden. Make sure the oil doesn't get so hot that the garlic scorches. Remove from heat and add the lemon zest and juice.

Toss linguine with olive oil mixture, parsley, grated cheese, salt and pepper. Serve immediately.

SERVES 4 TO 6

pantry pasta

This recipe came to me one night as I cleaned out the pantry and fridge. It took me all of 10 minutes to put together. The anchovies are always in my fridge and I love sneaking them into sauces for that je ne sais quoi. For more depth in my chicken stocks, I roast the bones first, then follow the regular procedure (see page 42). This gives me a rich, dark stock with loads of flavour.

3 tbsp. olive oil (45 mL)

1 large onion, diced

2 oz. spicy pancetta (60 g), finely diced

2 large cloves garlic, chopped

1/2 to 3/4 tsp. chile flakes or 1 small fresh red chile, chopped

3/4 cup canned plum tomatoes, diced with juice (175 mL)

3 anchovies, finely chopped

1 can (14 oz./398 mL) Romano or pinto beans, drained and rinsed

1 cup roasted chicken stock (page 42) (250 mL)

salt and freshly cracked black pepper

1 lb. penne rigate (500 g)

1/2 small bunch fresh basil, chopped

1/2 small bunch fresh parsley, chopped

freshly grated Parmigiano-Reggiano to taste

In a large skillet, heat oil over medium heat. Cook onion and pancetta until onion is soft, about 4 minutes. Add the garlic and cook for 1 more minute, or until just golden. Add chile flakes, tomatoes, anchovies, beans and stock. Reduce heat to low and simmer, uncovered, until reduced by one third, 8 to 10 minutes. Season with salt and pepper.

Meanwhile, cook pasta in boiling salted water for about 10 minutes, or until al dente. Drain well and add to sauce. Sprinkle with basil and parsley and toss for a couple of minutes to blend flavours. Adjust seasoning and serve immediately with freshly grated Parmigiano-Reggiano.

SERVES 4 TO 6

grilled zucchini panini with fontina and peppers

If you can make a grilled cheese sandwich, you can make this smashing little grilled sandwich — the only sandwich in the book! I love the great contrast between the peppery greens and the creamy fontina.

3 medium zucchini, thinly sliced

2 orange peppers, quartered

1/4 cup extra virgin olive oil (60 mL)

salt and freshly cracked black pepper

1/4 cup chopped fresh basil (60 mL)

8 small panini

5 oz. fontina (140 g), sliced

1 bunch arugula

Preheat grill to high. Clean well to prevent sticking.

Toss zucchini and orange peppers with oil, salt and black pepper until well coated. Sprinkle with basil and toss again.

Grill peppers and zucchini for 3 to 4 minutes per side, or until lightly browned.

Cut panini in half but do not cut all the way through, keeping a hinge intact. Layer zucchini and peppers on bottom of panini. Top with fontina and arugula. Close bread.

Grill panini on the upper rack not too close to heat. Turn sandwich when bread is warm, after about 3 minutes. Repeat on other side. (As a precaution, you can wrap the sandwiches in foil and grill them so the bread does not burn.) Serve immediately.

SERVES 8

clams in spicy thai broth

Here's a chance to throw all the ingredients in one pot, cover with a lid and eat in 5 minutes. Okay, there's a bit of work first — you have to wash and scrub the clams — but if you serve it like I usually do, with a salad and crusty bread, it's a pretty low-maintenance meal. I highly suggest improvising away in this one.

2 lb. littleneck clams (1 kg)

1 orange

2 tbsp. vegetable oil (25 mL)

1 large onion, chopped

3 cloves garlic, thinly sliced

2 stalks lemon grass, white part only, finely sliced

1 Thai chile, finely chopped (if you like it hot, go for another chile)

1-inch piece ginger (2.5 cm), peeled and grated

several kaffir lime leaves or grated zest of 1 lime

juice of 1 lime

1 cup clam juice (250 mL)

1/2 cup Gewürztraminer or other dry white wine (125 mL)

1/2 cup coconut milk (125 mL)

salt and freshly cracked black pepper to taste

freshly chopped coriander, for garnish

Thai basil leaves, for garnish

Wash clams thoroughly several times under cold running water. Soak in cold water for 10 minutes to remove trace sand. Drain the clams.

While clams are soaking, remove zest from orange in long, thin strips. Juice the orange. Set aside zest and juice.

In a large deep skillet with lid, heat oil over medium-high heat. Sauté onion until soft, about 3 minutes. Add garlic, lemon grass, chile and ginger; sauté for 2 minutes. Add reserved orange juice and zest, lime leaves, lime juice, clam juice, wine, coconut milk, salt and pepper. Bring to a boil over high heat. Reduce heat to low and simmer broth until reduced by one third, about 5 minutes. Add the drained clams. Cover and simmer until clams open, about 5 minutes. Remove from heat and discard any clams that do not open.

Stir in the coriander. Garnish clams with Thai basil.

SERVES 4 TO 6

seed-crusted lamb chops with tomato chutney

For a dish that sounds so interesting, it's very quick to make and will earn you huge accolades. The flavours are a combination of the tangy and nutty from North Africa with a sweet spicy Indian blend. Serve these chops with rice or couscous. I have also served this chutney with grilled shrimp. Ma ma ma!

grated zest of 1 lime

1/2 tsp. cracked black pepper (2 mL)

1/2 tsp. coriander seeds (2 mL), coarsely cracked

1/4 tsp. cumin seeds (1 mL), coarsely cracked

1/4 tsp. ground sumac (1 mL) (optional)

6 small lamb loin chops

2 tbsp. olive oil (25 mL)

salt to taste

TOMATO CHUTNEY

1 tbsp. olive oil (15 mL)

1 large onion, chopped

2 cloves garlic, thinly sliced

1/2 tsp. chopped fresh ginger (2 mL)

4 large plum tomatoes, peeled and chopped

1 tbsp. brown sugar (15 mL)

1 tbsp. pomegranate molasses (15 mL)

1/4 tsp. coriander seeds (1 mL), coarsely cracked

1/4 tsp. cumin seeds (1 mL), coarsely cracked

pinch cayenne

salt to taste

juice of 1/2 lime

1 tbsp. chopped fresh coriander (15 mL)

In a medium bowl, combine lime zest, pepper, coriander seeds, cumin seeds and sumac. Toss lamb chops in spice mixture to coat well. Cover and refrigerate while you make the chutney.

In a large skillet, heat 1 tbsp. (15 mL) olive oil over medium-high heat. Sauté onion for 4 to 5 minutes, or until very soft and golden. Add the garlic and ginger, reduce heat to low and cook, stirring, for 3 more minutes, or until garlic is soft but not brown. Stir in tomatoes, sugar, pomegranate molasses, coriander seeds, cumin seeds, cayenne, salt and lime juice. Bring mixture to a boil. Reduce heat to low, cover and simmer until chutney is thick and most of the liquid has evaporated, about 20 minutes. Adjust seasoning. Remove from heat and stir in fresh coriander.

Preheat oven to 375°F.

In a large ovenproof skillet, heat 2 tbsp. (25 mL) oil over high heat. Sprinkle lamb with salt and sear chops for about 2 minutes per side. Transfer the skillet to the oven and cook lamb for 5 minutes more for medium-rare, or until done to your liking. Serve with the tomato chutney.

SERVES 2

sesame-crusted salmon

Although this recipe has three components and looks intimidating, in fact it's a snap, since all the parts can cook at the same time. I love the texture and slightly sweet flavour of sushi rice, but you can use any other kind of rice. The nutty and crisp ginger and sesame crust on the salmon alongside the tangy sauce makes this a knock-out dish.

3 tbsp. black sesame seeds (45 mL)
1 tbsp. grated fresh ginger (15 mL)
4 salmon fillets (each 6 oz./175 g)
salt and freshly cracked black pepper to taste
1 tbsp. vegetable oil (15 mL)

RICE
1 1/2 cups sushi rice (375 mL)
1 1/2 cups cold water (375 mL)
1 tbsp. rice wine vinegar (15 mL)
1 tsp. sugar (5 mL)

SAUCE
1 tbsp. sesame oil (15 mL)
1 tbsp. vegetable oil (15 mL)
1 sweet onion, thinly sliced
4 large shiitake mushrooms, stems discarded, sliced
1 red pepper, thinly sliced
2 tbsp. good-quality soy sauce (25 mL)
2 tbsp. rice wine vinegar (25 mL)
2 tbsp. barley malt or hoisin sauce (25 mL)
splash lime juice

Preheat oven to 375°F.

Rinse the sushi rice several times with cold water to decrease starch. Combine the rinsed rice and 1 1/2 cups (375 mL) cold water in a small saucepan. Bring to a boil and boil for 1 minute. Reduce to lowest heat and simmer 10 minutes. Cover securely and remove from heat. Let stand 5 minutes. Stir in vinegar and sugar with a wooden spoon.

Meanwhile, in a shallow plate combine the sesame seeds and ginger. Season salmon very lightly with salt and pepper. Dip the flesh side of each salmon fillet into the sesame seed mixture.

Heat oil in a large skillet on medium heat. When oil is hot but not smoking, sear the salmon, about 2 minutes per side. Transfer salmon, sesame side up, to a small roasting pan and bake for 10 minutes, or until just firm but still pink in the middle.

To make the sauce, wipe the skillet clean. Over high heat, heat sesame oil and vegetable oil. Sauté onion for 4 to 5 minutes, or until just soft. Add the shiitake mushrooms and sauté for about 3 minutes, or until mushrooms are golden and soft. Stir in the red pepper, soy sauce, vinegar, barley malt and lime juice; reduce heat to medium and simmer until sauce is glossy and peppers begin to soften. Adjust seasoning.

Serve sauce over salmon with sushi rice.

SERVES 4

red snapper with saffron and orange en papillote

This method of wrapping food in little parchment bundles keeps in moisture and flavour. The paper puffs up in a big ball, trapping in the steam and gently cooking the package. There is much room for playing here, as orange roughy, halibut or salmon can be prepared this way with Asian, Mediterranean or French flavours. I've also cooked chicken and even just vegetables this way. But make sure not to overpower the main player with too much competition.

1/4 cup extra virgin olive oil (60 mL)

4 red snapper fillets (each about 5 oz./140 g), skin on

salt and freshly cracked black pepper to taste

2 cloves garlic, thinly sliced

2 shallots, thinly sliced

grated zest and juice of 1 orange

several threads saffron

1 leek, white part only, cut into julienne strips

1 carrot, cut into julienne strips

small handful capers

4 sprigs fresh thyme

4 sprigs fresh tarragon

splash dry vermouth

Preheat oven to 350°F. Cut four 11-inch (25 cm) squares of parchment paper. Fold each sheet of parchment in half diagonally. Open and drizzle each with a little of the oil.

Place a snapper fillet on each sheet of parchment, next to the fold. Season with salt and pepper. Top each fillet evenly with garlic, shallots, orange zest, saffron, leek, carrot, capers, thyme and tarragon. Drizzle with remaining olive oil, a splash of orange juice and vermouth.

Seal the parcels by first folding over the empty half of parchment paper. Starting at one end, twist the edges of the paper to form a tight seal, working along the edge until you have a half-moon shape. Lay the parcels on a baking sheet.

Bake for 20 minutes, or until parcels puff. Transfer the parcels to a platter. Cut each package open using scissors and carefully pour the contents onto serving plates. Or, to really wow your guests, serve this the traditional way by cutting open the packages on individual plates at the table.

SERVES 4

lime-and-mint-crusted chicken breast

Fresh mint and pistachios were my inspiration for this quick chicken dish that explodes with flavour. If you can't find ground sumac, just throw in a squeeze of lime juice for that extra tang.

2 cloves garlic, minced

1 small Thai chile, minced

grated zest of 1 large lime

1/2 cup chopped fresh mint (125 mL)

1/4 cup coarsely ground unsalted, unroasted pistachios or almonds (60 mL)*

1/2 tsp. ground sumac (2 mL)

4 boneless skinless chicken breasts (each 5 oz./140 g)

salt and freshly cracked black pepper to taste

2 tbsp. olive oil (25 mL)

Preheat oven to 375°F.

Combine garlic, chile, lime zest, mint, pistachios and sumac in a small bowl. Stir well.

Season chicken very lightly with salt and pepper. Heat oil in a large skillet over high heat. When oil is hot, sear the chicken for about 1 minute per side, or until golden. Dip both sides of chicken into pistachio mixture, patting down to create a crust. Transfer chicken to a small roasting pan and bake for 10 to 12 minutes, or until the juices run clear.

Serve with rice or couscous.

SERVES 4

* Coarsely grind the nuts in a food processor for the best texture.

red snapper with saffron and orange en papillote, p. 79

guine with lemon, olive oil and toasted garlic, p. 73

vietnamese grilled flank steak, p. 106; roasted sweet potatoes and apples, p.

spicy oven-baked chicken wings

Because I'm not generally a big fan of fried chicken wings, I bake these yummy ones. They're in the medium spice category. To get them to suicide, double the Jamaican hot sauce.

16 chicken wings

2 cloves garlic, minced

1/4 cup soy sauce (60 mL)

2 tbsp. hoisin sauce (25 mL)

1 tbsp. minced fresh ginger (15 mL)

1/2 tsp. paprika (2 mL)

1/4 tsp. cayenne (1 mL)

2 tbsp. hot sauce (preferably Jamaican) (25 mL)

chopped fresh coriander to taste

Preheat oven to 425°F. Line a baking sheet with parchment paper or well-oiled foil.

With a knife, remove wing tips from chicken wings and cut through the joint to separate into drumsticks and wing ends. Combine the garlic, soy sauce, hoisin sauce, ginger, paprika and cayenne in a medium bowl. Add the chicken wings and toss to coat well.

Remove wings from the sauce, reserving any leftover sauce. Arrange wings in a single layer on baking sheet. Bake for about 30 minutes, or until chicken is cooked through, brushing with reserved sauce if wings seem to be drying out.

Combine hot sauce and coriander in a large bowl. Add wings and toss to coat well. Serve immediately.

SERVES 4 OR 3 OR 2

baked pear with roquefort and port

This is the cheese course that eats like a dessert. You can whip it in the oven while you put some water on the boil for a simple pasta dish, and dinner is set. I wouldn't worry about following precise quantities. After all, the dish is just pears drizzled with sweet port and some sort of blue cheese crumbled to fill the middle. Super-easy and quick!

2 firm ripe pears (preferably Forelle or Bosc)
1/3 cup port (75 mL)
1/4 cup blue cheese (preferably Danish Blue) (60 mL), crumbled
3 tbsp. chopped hazelnuts (45 mL)

Preheat oven to 375°F.

Leave the skin on the pears. Core the pears using an apple corer or small knife. Stand pears in a small baking dish and drizzle with port. Bake for 25 to 30 minutes, or until pears are golden and just begin to soften. If the glaze begins to dry out, cover pan with foil. Port should be syrupy.

Remove pears from pan and fill cores with cheese. Arrange pears on serving plates and spoon the port glaze over each pear. Sprinkle with chopped nuts.

SERVES 2

essentials

Look no further if you want recipe
that have a little **more substance** than those
in the previous chapter. I'm talking about
food that you just can't live without.
You'll find everything from The Perfect Sala
and Chicken Stuffed with Pecorino and Chorizo
to Charred Tomato Soup and Vietnamese Grille
Flank Steak. These recipes will become part of
your own repertoire, and soon you'll be
adding your personal touches
As in the previous chapter, these recipes
feature interesting ingredients,
which are my signature.

apple and napa slaw with toasted almonds

I am not a big fan of coleslaws with a creamy base, so here's my offering without any mayonnaise. I use the milder napa cabbage and toasted almonds. The fennel seeds and the fresh mint give the slaw a smooth, peppery taste yet with some sweet notes.

DRESSING

1/4 cup chopped fresh mint (60 mL)

1/4 cup rice wine vinegar (60 mL)

2 tbsp. grape seed or olive oil (25 mL)

2 tsp. honey (10 mL)

1 1/2 tsp. fennel seeds (7 mL), toasted and ground

1 tsp. grated fresh ginger (5 mL)

1/2 tsp. Dijon mustard (2 mL)

grated zest and juice of 1 orange

pinch cayenne

SLAW

2 McIntosh apples, unpeeled

1 small head napa cabbage, core removed, finely sliced

chopped chives to taste

1/3 cup almonds (75 mL), toasted and coarsely chopped

In a large bowl, whisk together all the dressing ingredients.

Thinly slice the apples and add to the dressing with the cabbage and chives; toss well.

Cover and refrigerate for 1 to 2 hours before serving. Just before serving, sprinkle with almonds.

SERVES 10 TO 12

caesar salad with no-egg caesar dressing

These days we hear so much conflicting advice about using raw eggs that I thought I'd give you an eggless Caesar dressing that is still loaded with flavour. Don't even think of leaving out the anchovy.

DRESSING

2 to 3 cloves garlic, minced

1 anchovy, finely minced, or 1 tsp. anchovy paste (5 mL)

2 tbsp. red wine vinegar (25 mL)

1 tsp. Dijon mustard (5 mL)

1/2 tsp. Worcestershire sauce (2 mL)

splash Tabasco sauce

juice of 1/2 lemon

freshly cracked black pepper

1/2 cup extra virgin olive oil (125 mL)

1/4 cup grated Parmesan cheese (50 mL)

CROUTONS

4 slices baguette, cut into 1/2-inch (1 cm) cubes

3 tbsp. extra virgin olive oil (45 mL)

1 clove garlic, minced

2 heads romaine lettuce, torn into pieces

3 slices pancetta or bacon, pan-fried until crisp, crumbled

To make the dressing, combine the garlic, anchovy, vinegar, mustard, Worcestershire sauce, Tabasco, lemon juice and pepper in a food processor; pulse until smooth. In a slow, steady stream, pour in olive oil while processor is on. Add half of the Parmesan and pulse once or twice to blend. Adjust the seasoning. Set aside.*

Preheat oven to 375°F. Toss the bread cubes with olive oil and garlic until well coated. Spread on a baking sheet and toast in oven for 6 to 8 minutes, or until golden. Set aside to cool.

In a large bowl, toss the lettuce, dressing and croutons until well combined. Sprinkle with remaining Parmesan and the pancetta.

SERVES 8

❋ This dressing is not a regular emulsion because it doesn't contain an egg. When it sits, it will split. Don't worry — just give it a shake to blend it again.

the perfect salad

This recipe came about as I was browsing the produce aisle at Pusateri's — my favourite store and only the best on the planet. I was inspired. I thought baby spinach with a hit of fresh whole basil leaves and those tiny sweet bursting grape tomatoes would be such a great balance. To top it off I added some walnuts that I had roasted with tamari and corn syrup. Without exaggerating, this is the best salad I've ever made. That's why I call it the perfect salad. It takes a bit of time to make, but it isn't difficult, and it's worth it!

1/2 lb. cipollini or pearl onions (250 g), peeled

2 tbsp. olive oil (25 mL)

salt and freshly cracked black pepper to taste

1 pint grape or cherry tomatoes (500 mL)

1 bunch baby spinach (3 oz./75 g)

1 small head romaine lettuce

1 cup fresh basil leaves (250 mL)

TAMARI-GLAZED WALNUTS

1 tbsp. fennel seeds (15 mL), toasted and ground

1/2 tsp. anise seeds (2 mL), toasted and ground

1/4 tsp. cracked black pepper

1/4 cup tamari or other good-quality soy sauce (60 mL)

2 tbsp. corn syrup (25 mL)

1 cup walnut halves (250 mL)

DRESSING

1/3 cup extra virgin olive oil (75 mL)

2 tbsp. sherry vinegar (25 mL)

1 tsp. Worcestershire sauce (5 mL)

3/4 tsp. grainy mustard (4 mL)

1/2 tsp. honey (2 mL)

1/4 tsp. lemon zest (2 mL)

pinch dried oregano

salt and freshly cracked black pepper to taste

Preheat oven to 400°F.

In a medium bowl, toss cipollini with 1 tbsp. (15 mL) of the olive oil and season with salt and pepper. Transfer to a baking sheet. In the same bowl, toss tomatoes with remaining 1 tbsp. (15 mL) oil and season with salt and pepper. Transfer to a second baking sheet. Roast the cipollini for 10 minutes. Put the cherry tomatoes in the oven and continue to roast the vegetables for 15 minutes. Let tomatoes and cipollini cool. Cut the cipollini in quarters. Transfer cipollini and tomatoes to a bowl and set aside.

Turn oven down to 350°F. Line a baking sheet with parchment paper.

To make the glazed walnuts, in a small bowl, combine the fennel seeds, anise seeds and pepper. In another bowl, stir together the tamari and corn syrup. Stir in half of the spice mixture. Add the walnuts and toss to coat with the glaze. Spread the coated walnuts on the baking sheet. Bake on top rack for 35 minutes, or until glaze is almost dry but not burned. Remove the glazed walnuts from the oven and while still warm, dust with the remaining spice mixture. Let cool completely. Break nuts into pieces.

To make the dressing, in a bowl, whisk together the oil, vinegar, Worcestershire sauce, mustard, honey, lemon zest, oregano, salt and pepper. Adjust seasoning.

Cut or rip spinach, romaine and any large basil leaves into bite-sized pieces. Add them to the tomatoes and cipollini. Toss with the dressing. Serve the salad garnished with the glazed walnuts.

SERVES 4

charred tomato soup

This is probably the most amazing tomato soup I have ever made. Charring the tomatoes adds so much smoky depth to the flavour without a whole lot of other ingredients getting in the way. The touch of balsamic vinegar gives this soup a sweet and sour note that is almost subliminal. I've sometimes made this soup with cream, but I find it's deliciously rich enough without it.

4 large plum tomatoes

4 large field tomatoes

3 tbsp. olive oil (45 mL)

2 cloves garlic, quartered lengthwise

1 large onion, chopped

1 leek, white part only, thoroughly washed and chopped

1 yellow pepper, diced

1 tbsp. balsamic vinegar (15 mL)

4 cups chicken stock (1 L)

1 tsp. dried oregano (preferably Greek) (5 mL)

leaves from 1/2 bunch fresh basil, chopped

salt and freshly cracked black pepper to taste

GARNISH

baguette toasts

sliced Saint André or Camembert cheese

Preheat grill to high.

Grill tomatoes for 8 to 10 minutes, or until smoking, skins are beginning to char and middle feels soft. Remove from grill and purée in a food processor. Press purée through a coarse-mesh strainer set over a bowl and discard skins and seeds.

Combine the olive oil and garlic in a large saucepan over low heat. Cover and cook garlic for about 10 minutes, or until softened. Remove from heat and mash garlic in the pot with a fork. Add the onion, leek and yellow pepper. Cook over medium heat for 5 to 6 minutes, or until just soft.

Add the vinegar, stock, oregano and the puréed tomatoes. Bring to a boil, reduce heat to low and simmer, covered, for 30 minutes, stirring occasionally. Remove lid and simmer a further 15 to 20 minutes, or until soup is slightly thickened. Stir in basil and season with salt and pepper.

Serve with thin slices of toasted baguette topped with cheese.

SERVES 6

georgia's lemon artichokes

My mom has been making these artichokes since I could walk. I use the word "recipe" loosely because she has never actually written anything down. When it comes to quantities, she strictly works by instinct. But since that doesn't help you much, I thought I'd give you my rendition, and you can always make your own adjustments. The artichokes take some practice to clean, but they are well worth the effort.

10 small artichokes*	2 carrots, cut into 1-inch (2.5 cm) slices
1 1/2 lemons	4 new potatoes, peeled and quartered
1 cup water (250 mL)	salt and freshly cracked black pepper to taste
2 tbsp. all-purpose flour (25 mL)	3 green onions, chopped
1/4 cup olive oil (60 mL)	1/3 cup chopped fresh dill (75 mL) or to taste
1 onion, chopped	

To prepare artichokes, have a large bowl of water close at hand. Slice one lemon in half. Squeeze juice of 1/2 lemon into the water. Set aside another 1/2 lemon for the sauce. While trimming artichokes, rub generously with remaining 1/2 lemon to prevent browning. With your hands, pull off one third of the outer leaves. Cut off the bottom third of the stem, and trim away about half of the stem's tough exterior until you get to the tender middle. Cut off the top one third of the artichoke. Cut away any spiny tips that remain. Trim leaves from the bottom of artichoke where the stem meets the base and then remove the tough outer green skin. Transfer to the bowl.

In a medium bowl combine the water, flour and juice of reserved 1/2 lemon. Stir well to dissolve flour. Lift artichokes from soaking water and transfer to lemon-flour water; turn to coat.

In a medium saucepan, heat oil over medium-high heat. Sauté onion until soft and golden, 3 to 4 minutes. Add artichokes with lemon-flour water, carrots and potatoes; stir well. Season with salt and pepper.

Reduce heat to medium and bring to a boil, stirring to prevent flour from scorching. Reduce heat to low and simmer, partly covered, for 30 to 35 minutes, or until artichokes and potatoes are tender. Stir in the green onions and dill; adjust seasoning. Serve immediately.

SERVES 4

✳ If using larger artichokes, remove the choke — the purple prickly stuff in the centre — before cooking. Increase the cooking time.

baby bok choy with stir-fried shiitake mushrooms

The sky's the limit with this stir-fry. I prefer using baby bok choy because it's tender and easy to clean, but you can use the larger one or even broccoli, or any other green for that matter. Stir-fries are your easiest opportunity to be fearless in the kitchen. I always suggest chopping all your veggies before even thinking of turning the stove on.

1 tsp. sesame oil (5 mL)

1 tbsp. vegetable or safflower oil (15 mL)

1 onion, coarsely chopped

1 clove garlic, coarsely chopped

1 tsp. grated fresh ginger (5 mL)

1 red pepper, sliced

1 yellow pepper, sliced

1 cup sugar snap peas (250 mL)

6 shiitake mushrooms, stems discarded

2 baby bok choy, cut in half

3 tbsp. good-quality soy sauce (45 mL)

1 tsp. honey (5 mL)

black sesame seeds, for garnish

Heat sesame oil and vegetable oil in a large wok over high heat until almost smoking. Add the onion and stir-fry for 1 minute, or until soft. Add the garlic, ginger, red and yellow peppers and peas. Toss for 2 minutes, or until peppers are just beginning to soften. Add the mushrooms; continue to toss over high heat for 2 minutes. Add bok choy, soy sauce and honey. Cover for 1 to 2 minutes to steam bok choy.

Serve sprinkled with sesame seeds.

SERVES 4

roasted sweet potatoes and apples

The success of this simple side dish hinges on the quality of the curry powder you use. I'm not usually an advocate of prepared spices — I like to combine my own — but when you can find good-quality prepared curry powders or pastes they do save a ton of time. Ethnic varieties are usually better than the generic bottled brands, and I don't buy large amounts because their flavour dissipates quickly. You'll be thrilled with the tangy combination of apples and soft sweet potatoes.

2 tbsp. butter (25 mL)

2 medium sweet potatoes, cut into 1-inch (2.5 cm) cubes

2 medium Granny Smith or Mutsu (Crispin) apples, unpeeled, cubed

1 red onion, cut into 8 pieces

juice of 1 lime

1/2 tsp. good-quality Madras curry powder (2 mL)

pinch ground allspice

salt and pepper to taste

Preheat oven to 400°F.

Put the butter in a large roasting pan. Heat pan in oven until butter is melted and hot, about 1 minute. Add the sweet potatoes, apples, onion, lime juice, curry powder, allspice, salt and pepper. Toss well. Bake, shaking the pan a few times to prevent scorching, for 25 to 30 minutes, or until a knife sticks slightly when inserted.

SERVES 4 TO 6

spring farfalle with shiitake mushrooms and asparagus

When developing this brightly coloured and textured pasta dish, I was thinking of spring on a plate. Any mushroom, any green vegetable and almost any white wine will work. In fact, you could make this in the fall without the asparagus and play more on the earthy wild mushroom flavour. Pasta dishes are a good springboard for taking some chances with a recipe. Keep the intense flavours of the recipe, like the lemon, stock, vermouth, shallots and herbs, and change the other variables.

2 tbsp. olive oil (25 mL)	juice of 1/2 lemon
4 shallots, quartered	2 cups good-quality chicken or veal stock (500 mL)
2 sprigs fresh thyme	1/2 cup dry vermouth (125 mL)
1/2 lb. asparagus (250 g), trimmed	1 cup fresh or frozen green peas (250 mL)
2 tbsp. butter (25 mL)	1 lb. farfalle (bowtie pasta) (500 g)
6 shiitake mushrooms, stems discarded, sliced	chopped fresh tarragon (optional)
1 large clove garlic, chopped	salt and freshly cracked black pepper
grated zest of 1 lemon	freshly grated Grana Padano to taste

Preheat oven to 375°F.

In a small roasting pan, gently toss the oil, shallots and thyme. Roast, stirring frequently, for 15 to 17 minutes, or until shallots are golden and soft. Discard the thyme and set aside.

Blanch the asparagus in boiling salted water for 2 minutes. Immerse immediately in cold water to stop the cooking. Drain well, pat dry and cut into thirds. Set aside.

In a large skillet, melt the butter over high heat. Sauté the mushrooms, tossing, until golden, about 2 minutes. Add the garlic and the roasted shallots; sauté for 2 minutes, or until garlic is just golden. Add the lemon zest, lemon juice, stock and vermouth. Bring to a boil. Reduce heat to low and simmer, uncovered, until reduced by half, about 8 minutes. Stir in the peas and asparagus and simmer for 2 minutes, or until peas are cooked.

Meanwhile, cook pasta in boiling salted water for 8 to 10 minutes, or until al dente. Drain (do not rinse) and toss with sauce. Sprinkle with chopped tarragon (if using) and season with salt and pepper to taste. Serve immediately with freshly grated Grana Padano.

SERVES 4 TO 6

veggie burgers with tahini sauce

I just want to say off the bat that these are not the usual hockey-puck veggie burgers made with tofu or tempeh. I wanted to make a flavourful burger that is soft inside and tastes great in a pita with tahini sauce. These burgers hold together well with their crispy exterior, but the middle is a little soft. Handle them carefully when you place them in the pitas.

1 can (14 oz./398 mL) chickpeas, drained and rinsed

1 medium sweet potato, peeled

1 medium zucchini

1/4 cup + 2 tbsp. olive oil (60 mL + 25 mL)

1 small onion, chopped

1 small leek, white and light green parts only,
    washed well and chopped

1 green onion, chopped

1 clove garlic, chopped

1 egg white

2 tbsp. cornmeal (25 mL)

1 1/2 tbsp. cornstarch (20 mL)

1 tbsp. chopped fresh basil (15 mL)

salt and freshly cracked black pepper to taste

TAHINI SAUCE

1 clove garlic, minced

juice of 1/2 lemon

1/4 cup tahini (60 mL)

1/4 cup water (60 mL)

1 tbsp. chopped fresh parsley (15 mL)

salt and freshly cracked black pepper to taste

In a food processor, purée the chickpeas. Transfer to a medium bowl. In the food processor or by hand, grate the sweet potato. Pat dry on paper towels and add to the chickpeas. Grate the zucchini. Squeeze dry in a kitchen towel, removing as much moisture as possible. Add to the chickpeas.

In a medium saucepan, heat 2 tbsp. (25 mL) of the oil over medium-high heat. Sauté the onion, leek, green onion and garlic until soft, about 4 minutes. Add the cooked vegetables to the chickpeas. Stir in the egg white, cornmeal, cornstarch, basil, salt and pepper. Shape into 6 patties. Refrigerate until ready to cook.

To make the tahini sauce, in a small bowl stir together the garlic, lemon juice, tahini, water, parsley, salt and pepper.

In a large nonstick skillet over medium heat, heat the remaining 1/4 cup (60 mL) oil until hot. Fry the patties, three at a time, for about 4 minutes per side, or until crisp and firm to the touch. Drain on paper towels.

Carefully transfer the burgers to toasted pitas and drizzle with the tahini sauce.

SERVES 6

latin frittata

A frittata is just a fancy word for an omelette that's baked in the oven. They're quick, easy and infinitely variable, which makes them great for a quick dinner. This one uses Latin ingredients like chorizo sausage, potatoes and sherry, but feel free to have fun by using just about anything you have in the fridge or pantry.

2 medium Yukon Gold potatoes

4 tbsp. olive oil (60 mL)

2 medium Portobello mushrooms, stems discarded, diced

1 fresh chorizo sausage, casing removed, chopped

2 green onions, chopped

2 cloves garlic, chopped

1 tbsp. chopped fresh thyme (15 mL)

6 large eggs

2 tbsp. dry sherry (25 mL)

salt and freshly cracked black pepper to taste

3 oz. firm goat cheese, crumbled (75 g)

In a medium saucepan, boil the potatoes in salted water until just fork-tender. Drain and let cool. Peel and dice the potatoes. Transfer to a bowl.

Preheat oven to 375°F.

Heat 2 tbsp. (25 mL) of the oil in 10-inch (25 cm) skillet on medium heat. Cook mushrooms, stirring frequently, until browned. Add to the potatoes. Add 1 tbsp. (15 mL) of the oil to the skillet. Cook the chorizo until browned and cooked through, 3 to 4 minutes. Stir in the green onions and garlic; cook, stirring, until soft, about 2 minutes. Add to the potatoes. Stir in the thyme.

Coat the bottom and sides of the skillet with the remaining 1 tbsp. (15 mL) oil and heat on low heat.

In a medium bowl, whisk the eggs and sherry until just foamy. Add the potato mixture and stir to combine. Season with salt and pepper.

Immediately pour the egg mixture into the skillet. Cook the frittata until the edges start to get firm, about 4 minutes. Sprinkle with goat cheese and bake for 15 minutes, or until firm but still moist in the centre.

Remove frittata from oven and let sit for 2 or 3 minutes. Loosen the frittata from the pan with a spatula and flip it out onto a serving platter or cutting board.

SERVES 4

spanish rice with sherry sautéed shrimp

This dish can have so many incarnations that it's perfect for calling it your own. You can add different kinds of beans, change the rice, make it spicy — whatever you want. If I'm in the mood for something tropical, I replace half the liquid with coconut milk.

1 tbsp. olive oil (15 mL)

1 large onion, finely chopped

2 cloves garlic, minced

1/2 green pepper, finely diced

1/2 red pepper, finely diced

several threads saffron

1 tsp. dried oregano (5 mL)

1/2 tsp. cumin seeds (2 mL), ground

1/4 tsp. cayenne (1 mL)

4 plum tomatoes, diced

salt and freshly cracked black pepper

1 3/4 cups chicken or vegetable stock or water (425 mL)

1 cup basmati rice (250 mL), rinsed well in warm water

1 cup cooked or drained canned pinto beans (250 mL)

SHRIMP

2 tbsp. olive oil (25 mL)

1 clove garlic, thinly sliced

1 onion, thinly sliced

12 large shrimp, peeled, deveined, tails on

salt and pepper to taste

3 plum tomatoes, peeled and diced

1/3 cup dry sherry (75 mL)

1/4 cup chopped fresh parsley (60 mL)

In a medium saucepan, heat oil over medium heat. Cook onion, stirring frequently, for 3 to 4 minutes, or until soft. Stir in garlic, green pepper, red pepper, saffron, oregano, cumin and cayenne. Cook, stirring, for 3 minutes, or until peppers are just soft. Add the tomatoes and season with salt and pepper. Cook, stirring frequently, just until tomatoes soften, about 3 minutes. Add the stock. Increase heat to high and bring to a boil. Stir in rice and beans. Reduce heat to low, cover and simmer for 12 minutes. Remove from heat and let stand for 5 minutes. Fluff with a fork.

While rice is cooking, cook the shrimp. In a large skillet, heat the oil over medium heat. Cook the garlic and onion, stirring frequently, until onion is just soft. Add the shrimp, salt and pepper. Increase heat to high and toss for 2 minutes, or until shrimp are just opaque. Stir in the tomatoes and sherry. Simmer for 1 to 2 minutes, or until most of the liquid has evaporated and shrimp are just tender. Remove from heat and sprinkle with parsley. Serve over the rice.

SERVES 4

seed-crusted shrimp with orange, black olive and mint salad

Once you taste these shrimp, you'll put it at the top of your list of "can't live without" meals. They are a little taste of Morocco with minimal effort. North African cuisine is an incredible way to experience the contrast of many flavours on the palate. Together, the shrimp and salad cover it all — salty, sweet, sour and spicy. This is the perfect recipe for showing how fearless you can be in the kitchen. And don't even think about using dried mint in place of the fresh. Fresh is the only way to go.

SALAD

3 large navel oranges, peeled and segmented

1 red onion, thinly sliced

1 clove garlic, minced

1/3 cup cured black olives (75 mL)

1/4 cup chopped fresh mint (60 mL)

1/4 cup olive oil (60 mL)

1 tbsp. sherry vinegar (15 mL)

freshly cracked black pepper to taste

SHRIMP

1 lb. large shrimp (about 18) (500 g), peeled, deveined, tails on

1 tbsp. olive oil (15 mL)

1/2 tsp. coriander seeds (2 mL), coarsely cracked

1 tsp. cumin seeds (5 mL), coarsely cracked

grated zest of 1 lime

1/4 cup chopped fresh coriander (60 mL)

coarse salt to taste

coarsely cracked black pepper to taste

Combine all salad ingredients in a medium bowl. Toss well. Let stand for about 1 hour before serving for best flavour.

To make the shrimp, preheat grill to high. Rub shrimp with oil. In a small bowl, combine the coriander seeds, cumin seeds, lime zest, fresh coriander, salt and pepper. Coat shrimp with spice blend. Refrigerate until ready to cook. Grill shrimp for 2 to 3 minutes per side, or until shrimp start to curl and turn pink.

Serve shrimp over the salad.

SERVES 4

harissa-baked rainbow trout

Harissa is a Tunisian chile paste that rocks. Although you can buy it in some North African stores, homemade is superior. I have seen a number of variations, but usually it is a combination of mint or coriander, garlic, loads of olive oil and mild chiles. It's got a bit of a bite, but the herbs and garlic really come through. I use it on everything from lamb to beef to chicken. If you want to use it on other seafood, choose something hearty, like salmon or shrimp.

HARISSA

2 medium dried New Mexico chiles

3 cloves garlic, minced

1/4 cup extra virgin olive oil (60 mL)

1 tsp. honey (5 mL)

3/4 tsp. cumin seeds (4 mL), ground

1/2 tsp. coriander seeds (2 mL), ground

1/4 cup chopped fresh coriander or mint (60 mL)

TROUT

2 medium whole rainbow trout, cleaned, or 1 large (1 1/2-lb./750 g) trout

salt

2 tbsp. olive oil (25 mL)

1 tbsp. vegetable oil (15 mL)

1/2 lemon

To make the harissa, soak the chiles in hot water for 30 minutes. Drain well and chop. Combine with garlic, oil, honey, cumin seeds and coriander seeds in a small food processor. Pulse until smooth. Add the coriander and pulse to combine.

Brush the cavity and outside of trout with harissa. Season with salt.

Preheat oven to 350°F.

Heat the olive and vegetable oils in a large ovenproof skillet on high heat. Fry fish for about 2 minutes per side or until golden. Transfer skillet to oven and bake for 6 to 8 minutes for 2 smaller trout or 12 to 14 minutes for 1 large trout. Fish is cooked when flesh is firm but meat comes away from bone. Remove from oven and squeeze lemon juice over fish.

SERVES 4

pan-seared cod in a spinach reduction

Cod has such a rich flavour of its own that it doesn't need a lot of extra help, so I've matched it up with a simple spinach, cream and nutmeg combination. The spinach makes this dish ideal for spring, but it works well any time of year. If you feel like being adventurous in the spring, use sorrel instead of spinach. Sorrel has a uniquely tangy hit that nothing can compare to. It's available for a month or so in late spring.

1 bunch spinach, washed thoroughly and tough stems removed

1 tbsp. vegetable oil (15 mL)

4 cod fillets (each 6 oz./175 g)

salt and pepper to taste

1 tbsp. butter (15 mL)

1/2 cup whipping (35%) cream (125 mL)

1/4 cup finely chopped green onions (60 mL)

chopped leaves from a couple of sprigs fresh dill

salt and cracked black pepper

pinch freshly grated nutmeg

1/2 lemon

Preheat oven to 350°F.

Blanch the spinach in boiling salted water for 2 minutes or just until it softens. Drain and rinse under cold water to stop cooking. With your hands, squeeze out as much liquid as possible. Finely chop spinach and set aside.

Heat oil in a medium ovenproof skillet over high heat. Season cod with salt and pepper and sear it for 1 minute per side or until golden. Transfer skillet to oven and bake for 7 to 8 minutes for each inch (2.5 cm) of thickness of fish.

Meanwhile, in a small saucepan, melt the butter. Add cream and the chopped spinach; bring to a boil. Stir in green onions, dill, salt, pepper and nutmeg. Simmer for 1 minute just to develop flavour. For a thicker sauce, simmer a few minutes longer.

Pour some sauce onto 4 plates and lay cooked fish over sauce. Spoon some sauce over the fish and drizzle with the juice of half a lemon.

SERVES 4

homemade crispy chicken fingers with plum sauce

I found the trick to making great homemade chicken fingers — use dark meat instead of white. It has tons more flavour and it's almost impossible to dry out. This is great for kids but just as delicious for us adults. I include my recipe for the plum sauce because I haven't found a store-bought product that isn't lame.

PLUM SAUCE

1 tbsp. vegetable oil (15 mL)

1 small onion, finely chopped

1/2 cup plum jam (125 mL)

2 tbsp. rice wine vinegar (25 mL)

1 tbsp. tamari soy sauce (15 mL)

1 1/2 tsp. Dijon mustard (7 mL)

1/4 tsp. Worcestershire sauce (1 mL), or to taste

juice of 1/2 lime

few drops Tabasco, or to taste

CHICKEN FINGERS

4 boneless skinless chicken thighs

salt and freshly cracked black pepper to taste

3 large eggs

1 cup cornmeal (250 mL)

1 tsp. dried oregano (5 mL)

1/2 tsp. cayenne (2 mL)

1/2 cup all-purpose flour (125 mL)

1 cup coarsely ground corn flakes (250 mL)

1/4 cup vegetable oil (60 mL)

To make the sauce, in a small saucepan over medium-low heat, heat the oil. Cook onion, stirring frequently, for 3 minutes, or until soft. Add the jam, vinegar, tamari, mustard, Worcestershire sauce, lime juice and Tabasco. Cook, stirring, over medium heat for 2 to 5 minutes, or until jam is melted and mixture has come to a boil. Remove from heat. Serve warm or at room temperature.

Preheat oven to 350°F.

Slice chicken thighs lengthwise into strips as thick or thin as you like. Season with salt and pepper. In a shallow dish, lightly beat the eggs. In a second shallow dish, stir together the cornmeal, oregano and cayenne. Have ready in two separate shallow dishes the flour and corn flakes. Have ready a plate to transfer the coated chicken fingers to.

Dip a chicken strip first in the flour, then in the egg, then in the cornmeal, in the egg again and finally in the corn flakes. Press the corn flakes firmly so they adhere. Transfer to the plate and repeat with remaining chicken strips.

Pour oil into a large skillet and heat over high until hot but not smoking. Fry chicken fingers, in batches if necessary, for 2 minutes per side or until golden. Transfer to a baking sheet. Bake until chicken is no longer pink inside and is firm to the touch, 9 to 10 minutes depending on thickness of chicken fingers. Serve chicken fingers with plum sauce.

SERVES 4

chicken stuffed with pecorino and chorizo

Talk about the perfect balance between looks and flavour. This chicken breast is stuffed with sharp pecorino (an Italian sheep's milk cheese) and spicy sausage. As if that wasn't enough, I wrapped it in pancetta for a crispy coating. Man, this chicken rules! I usually slice it across the grain to show off the beautiful filling. I serve it with a simple salad and a vegetable. It's so good I don't think it needs a starch to accompany it.

3 tbsp. olive oil (40 mL)

1 large shallot, finely chopped

1 clove garlic, finely chopped

1 fresh chorizo sausage, casing removed, crumbled

1 tsp. chopped fresh oregano (5 mL)

salt and pepper to taste

1 1/2 oz. pecorino (45 g), grated

2 tbsp. chopped fresh basil (25 mL)

4 boneless skinless chicken breasts

1 egg white, beaten

8 thin slices pancetta or bacon

In a medium saucepan, heat 1 tbsp. (15 mL) of the oil over medium-high heat. Sauté the shallot and garlic until golden, about 2 minutes. Add the sausage; cook, stirring frequently, until meat is browned, about 5 minutes. Stir in oregano, salt and pepper. Remove from heat and let cool completely.

Preheat oven to 350°F.

Add pecorino and basil to cheese mixture. Season with salt and pepper. Stir well with a wooden spoon until mixture is combined.

Cut a slit straight down into each chicken breast running the length of the breast but not all the way through it (imagine it like a zippered pouch). Fill each breast with 1 to 2 tbsp. (15 to 25 mL) of stuffing. Brush the slit with egg white to seal the opening and prevent filling from oozing out. Sprinkle chicken with salt and pepper. Wrap each breast with 2 slices of pancetta. Tie with butcher's twine to secure the pancetta around the chicken.

In a medium skillet over high heat, heat the remaining 2 tbsp. (25 mL) of the oil until hot but not smoking. Sear chicken until golden, about 2 minutes per side. Transfer chicken to a roasting pan and bake for 12 to 15 minutes, or until juices run clear and a small knife inserted into the middle of the breast is warm to the touch.

SERVES 4

roasted turkey breast with niagara riesling and pancetta

This recipe took shape when I was dreaming of France, Alsace in particular. There's something so soothing about the combination of apples, Riesling and crunchy pancetta. (Okay, so I detoured to Italy with the pancetta, but if I'm in Europe anyway, I might as well travel.) Besides, it gives you a reason to cook turkey any night of the week. This stunning dish is simple to execute. Use a meat thermometer to check that the turkey is cooked through.

2 tbsp. clarified butter (25 mL)*	2 slices pancetta or bacon, chopped
1 boneless skinless turkey breast (1 1/2 lb./750 g)	2 cloves garlic, thinly sliced
salt and cracked black pepper to taste	1 Mutsu (Crispin) or Granny Smith apple, sliced
leaves from 3 sprigs fresh thyme, chopped	1 cup chicken stock (250 mL)
3 or 4 leaves fresh sage, chopped	1/2 cup Niagara Riesling (125 mL)
6 shallots, quartered	1/2 cup whipping (35%) cream (125 mL)

Preheat oven to 375°F.

In a large ovenproof skillet, melt butter over high heat. Season turkey with salt and pepper; sprinkle with half the thyme and sage. Sear turkey for about 2 minutes per side, or until golden. Remove turkey from pan and set aside.

Return the pan to medium heat. Add shallots, pancetta and garlic. Cook until shallots are just translucent and pancetta is golden, 3 to 4 minutes. Add the apple slices and toss for 2 minutes just to soften apples. Stir in the remaining thyme and sage, the stock and Riesling. Lay turkey breasts over the mixture.

Transfer skillet to oven and roast for 30 to 35 minutes, or until a thermometer inserted in the thickest part of the breast reads 175°F.

Remove turkey from pan and cover loosely with foil. Add cream to skillet and bring to a boil over high heat, stirring. Simmer, stirring occasionally, until liquid is reduced by half and slightly thickened. Slice the turkey, arrange on plates and spoon sauce over top.

SERVES 4 TO 6

✳ Clarified butter is butter from which the milk solids have been removed to prevent it from burning. Using clarified butter gives a rich, sweeter flavour to this turkey. To make: melt 1/2 lb. (250 g) unsalted butter in a small saucepan over very low heat for 20 to 30 minutes, or until solids collect and adhere to bottom of pan. Skim top of any foam and strain butter through a cheesecloth. Refrigerate butter and use as needed.

five-spice pork tenderloin with mango pomegranate chutney

I have fallen in love with Chinese five-spice powder. I whip up a little batch, leaving the seeds whole, store it in an airtight container and then just grind some when I need it. I have found this spice blend adds an interesting floral and spicy range to Asian recipes. The five spice flavours work amazingly with sweet accompaniments like the Mango Pomegranate Chutney served with this pork. The Szechuan peppercorns and star anise can be a little tricky to find. Try your favourite Asian spice or grocery store. It's well worth the journey!

FIVE-SPICE POWDER

8 whole star anise

6 whole cloves

1 tbsp. Szechuan or black peppercorns (15 mL)

2 tsp. fennel seeds (10 mL)

2 tsp. cinnamon (10 mL)

MANGO POMEGRANATE CHUTNEY

1 tbsp. vegetable oil (15 mL)

1 large onion, chopped

2 cloves garlic, thinly sliced

1/2 tsp. finely chopped fresh ginger (2 mL)

1 ripe mango, diced

1 tbsp. brown sugar (15 mL)

1 tbsp. pomegranate molasses (15 mL)

1/4 tsp. coriander seeds (1 mL), coarsely ground

1/4 tsp. cumin seeds (1 mL), coarsely ground

pinch cayenne

salt to taste

juice of 1 lime

chopped fresh mint to taste

chopped fresh coriander to taste

2 pork tenderloins (each 3/4 lb./375 g)

2 tbsp. soy sauce (25 mL)

1 tbsp. five-spice powder (15 mL)

1 tbsp. grated fresh ginger (15 mL)

1 tbsp. vegetable oil (15 mL)

1 tsp. sesame oil (5 mL)

To make the five-spice powder, combine star anise, cloves, peppercorns and fennel seeds in a small skillet. Toss over medium heat for about 2 minutes or until lightly toasted and fragrant. Grind in a coffee grinder or with a mortar and pestle. Stir in the cinnamon. Set aside. (Store leftover spice in a sealed container.)

To make the chutney, in a large skillet, heat oil over medium-high heat. Sauté onion for 4 to 5 minutes, or until very soft and golden. Add the garlic and ginger, reduce heat to low and cook for 3 more minutes, or until garlic is soft but not brown. Stir in mango, sugar, pomegranate molasses, coriander seeds, cumin, cayenne, salt and lime juice. Increase heat to high and cook, stirring frequently, until mixture comes to a boil. Reduce heat to low, cover and simmer, stirring occasionally, for about 20 minutes, or until relish is thick and most of the liquid has evaporated. Adjust seasoning and set aside.

Preheat oven to 375°F.

Brush pork with soy sauce. Sprinkle with five-spice powder and grated ginger.

Heat a large ovenproof skillet over medium heat. Add the vegetable and sesame oils. When the oil is hot, sear the pork on all sides, about 3 minutes total. Transfer skillet to the oven and roast pork for 15 minutes, 30 mins. or until juicy and moist and a meat thermometer reads at least 165°F.

Stir mint and fresh coriander into chutney. Serve pork with chutney.

SERVES 4 TO 6

vietnamese grilled flank steak

It's a shame that most of us try flank steak only when we're at our favourite bistro. That's exactly why I include it as one of my essentials. It's an inexpensive cut of meat that has a ton of flavour. To make it tender, though, you have to marinate it and cook it properly. Marinades traditionally contain something acidic (to tenderize and flavourize), some spice (for flavour) and something sweet (to balance the acid). I am so inspired by Vietnamese flavours that here I've given a traditional French dish a Southeast Asian swish. Try your hand at your own variation of this steak.

MARINADE

1 large onion, chopped

1 large jalapeño, seeded and chopped

2 cloves garlic, minced

juice of 2 limes

grated zest of 1 lime

1 cup dry sherry (250 mL)

5 tbsp. fish sauce (75 mL)

1 tbsp. black peppercorns (15 mL), coarsely cracked

1 tbsp. brown sugar (15 mL)

1 tbsp. grated fresh ginger (15 mL)

1 tbsp. hoisin sauce (15 mL)

1 tsp. whole cloves (5 mL)

1 tsp. coriander seeds (5 mL), crushed

1/2 tsp. allspice berries (2 mL)

1 flank steak (2 lb./1 kg)

several sprigs fresh Thai basil, chopped

several sprigs fresh coriander, chopped

salt and freshly cracked black pepper to taste

Combine marinade ingredients in a shallow baking dish or large resealable plastic bag. Immerse flank steak in marinade. Cover and refrigerate for at least 6 hours or up to 24 hours, turning steak occasionally.

Preheat grill to high.

Remove steak from marinade (discard the marinade) and season both sides of steak with Thai basil, fresh coriander, salt and pepper. Grill for 7 to 8 minutes per side for medium-rare. Remove steak from grill and let rest, covered loosely with foil, for 5 minutes. Thinly slice steak against the grain. Serve immediately.

SERVES 6 TO 8

herb-roasted rack of lamb with romesco sauce

Romesco is a rustic Spanish sauce that I introduced to my repertoire a few years ago. I've never looked back. It can be made ahead, kept in the fridge, then brought to room temperature just before serving. It has the texture of a thick, grainy mayonnaise, and the full flavour of the hazelnuts, garlic and roasted red peppers put it in my "must have" category.

1/2 cup chopped canned plum tomatoes
  (preferably San Marzano) (125 mL), drained

1 1/2 tbsp. olive oil (20 mL)

1 slice rustic bread

1/4 cup skinned whole hazelnuts (60 mL)

1 red pepper, roasted and peeled

2 cloves garlic, chopped

pinch cayenne

1/3 cup extra virgin olive oil (75 mL)

salt and freshly cracked black pepper to taste

lemon juice (optional)

2 large cloves garlic, minced

1/3 cup chopped mixed fresh herbs (such as rosemary, mint, oregano
  and thyme) (75 mL)

1/4 cup olive oil (60 mL)

salt and freshly cracked black pepper to taste

2 racks spring lamb (about 1.5 lb./750 g each), chine bone removed*

To make the romesco sauce, cook the tomatoes, stirring frequently, in a small saucepan over low heat until very dry, 6 to 8 minutes. Let cool. In a small skillet over medium-high heat, heat the oil. Fry the bread until golden on both sides. Let cool slightly. Wipe the skillet clean. In the same skillet, toast the hazelnuts until golden.

Purée the roasted red pepper in a food processor. Add the bread and the hazelnuts; pulse until smooth. Add the cooled tomatoes, the garlic and cayenne; pulse. With machine running, pour in the olive oil in a slow, steady stream until sauce is smooth. Do not overprocess or the sauce will split. Season with salt and pepper. Add a touch of lemon juice, if desired. Cover and set aside while you cook the lamb. (You can cook the sauce ahead and refrigerate it, covered. Bring it to room temperature before serving.) Put oven rack in the bottom of the oven. Preheat oven to 375°F. Heat a large roasting pan in the oven for 10 minutes.

Meanwhile, combine the garlic, herbs, oil, salt and pepper. Rub all over the lamb. Put the lamb in the hot roasting pan and roast for 10 minutes. Turn the racks and cook the other side another 10 minutes for medium-rare, or until a meat thermometer reads 145°F. Let racks rest for 5 minutes. Slice into chops and serve with romesco sauce.

SERVES 4 TO 6

✳ Ask your butcher to remove the chine bone (part of the backbone). It'll make racks easier to cut into chops.

roast leg of lamb greek style

For me, lamb is an absolute staple. Roasted leg of lamb is my equivalent of a Sunday roast beef dinner. I don't fuss with it at all, and the only prerequisite is that you load it with garlic and any combination of fresh chopped herbs your heart desires.

1/3 cup chopped mixed fresh herbs (such as thyme, dill and mint) (75 mL)
1/4 cup olive oil (60 mL)
juice of 1 lemon
4 cloves garlic, minced
salt and freshly cracked black pepper to taste
1 bone-in leg of lamb (3 to 4 lb./1.5 to 2 kg)

Preheat oven to 400°F.

In a medium bowl, combine the herbs, oil, lemon juice, garlic, salt and pepper. Put lamb on a rack in a large roasting pan. Brush lamb liberally with herb mixture.

Roast lamb for 30 minutes. Reduce heat to 350°F. Roast lamb, brushing it often with herb mixture, for 60 to 90 minutes more for medium, or until a meat thermometer reads 150°F.

SERVES 8 TO 10

simply
irresistible

When I talk about "simply irresistible" recipes, I mean those that make you feel *sooo* goo the instant you taste them. These are **memory-making dishes** that you'll want to share with **family and friends.** They are not necessarily more complicated they're just **irresistible in flavour** and will become some of your fast favourites. **Being fearless** doesn't just mean cooking something that's difficult. It is bei **fearless with your taste buds** and experimenting. Let me take you on an **adventure** of my fearless experiments — these recipes are th **joys of my culinary journeys.**

herb and reggiano crackers

Who says you can't make your own crackers at home in a snap? One day I had to come up with a new appetizer and I was inspired to make these crackers. The whole herbs make a beautiful pattern on the finished crispy cracker, and the cheese gives them a golden tone along with a distinct depth of flavour.

3/4 cup all-purpose flour (175 mL)

1/4 cup finely grated Parmigiano-Reggiano (60 mL)

1/4 tsp. baking soda (1 mL)

1/4 tsp. salt (1 mL)

1/4 tsp. cracked black pepper (1 mL)

2 tbsp. cold butter (25 mL), cut into small pieces

leaves from 2 sprigs fresh thyme, chopped

leaves from 2 sprigs fresh parsley, chopped

2 chives, finely chopped

leaves from 1 sprig parsley

1/3 cup buttermilk (75 mL)

1 egg white, whisked with 1 tsp. (5 mL) water

Line a baking sheet with parchment paper.

In a food processor, combine the flour, cheese, baking soda, salt and pepper; pulse a few times just to mix. Add the butter and pulse just until mixture resembles coarse meal. Transfer mixture to a bowl. Add the chopped herbs, whole parsley leaves and buttermilk. Stir until mixture just comes together. Don't overmix or the crackers will be tough instead of crisp and flaky.

Turn dough onto a well-floured surface. Knead several times until dough forms a ball. Dust lightly with flour if dough is too sticky. Roll out dough to 1/8-inch (3 mm) thickness. Using a crimped pastry wheel, cut dough into various-sized triangles and rectangles. Place crackers on baking sheet and refrigerate for 30 minutes.

Preheat oven to 375°F. Brush crackers with the eggwash. Bake for 17 to 20 minutes, or until browned and crisp. Cool on a rack. Serve with Kopanisti (see page 58) or your favourite spread.

MAKES ABOUT 30 CRACKERS, DEPENDING ON SIZE

grilled pizza with arugula, peppers and niçoise olives, p. 146

dark ale–battered halibut and chips, p. 156

chicken tacos with picante papaya mojo, p. 1

toasted-spice flat bread

With a touch of toasted spices and coarse salt added to a simple bread dough, this flat bread takes on its own nutty flavour that is evocative of the Middle East. The pizza stone helps to get that super-crisp texture, but if you don't own a stone you can easily bake these on a baking sheet.

1 1/4 cups hot water (300 mL)

1/2 cup whole-milk plain yogurt (125 mL)

1 tsp. sugar (5 mL)

1 pkg. active dry yeast

1 cup whole wheat bread flour (250 mL)

2 1/2 to 2 3/4 cups unbleached
    white bread flour (625 to 675 mL)

2 tsp. salt (10 mL)

3 tbsp. olive oil (45 mL), plus additional for brushing

coarse salt to taste

1/2 tsp. coarsely cracked cumin seeds (2 mL)

1/2 tsp. coarsely cracked coriander seeds (2 mL)

In a medium bowl, stir together the hot water, yogurt and sugar. Test temperature of liquid after adding yogurt to ensure it is just lukewarm, not hot. Whisk in the yeast. Let stand for about 5 minutes until the mixture is slightly foamy. Stir in the whole wheat flour and 1 cup (250 mL) of the white flour, stirring until dough is sponge-like. Cover and let stand in a warm place until doubled, 30 to 45 minutes.

Sprinkle the sponge with 2 tsp. (10 mL) salt, the oil and half the remaining flour. Turn onto a well-floured surface. Knead dough, adding flour as dough becomes too sticky to work, until dough is smooth and elastic, 6 to 8 minutes. The amount of flour needed will vary depending on humidity and other factors.

Clean and lightly oil the bowl. Return the dough to the bowl, cover and let stand in a warm place until doubled, about 1 1/2 hours.

Preheat oven to 425°F. Heat a pizza stone in the bottom third of the oven for 20 minutes, or according to manufacturer's instructions.

Punch down dough and divide into 6 equal rounds. Cover and let rest for 10 minutes.

On a lightly floured surface, roll each round into a rectangle about 1/4 inch (5 mm) thick. Brush off excess flour. With your fingers, press dimples into each rectangle. Brush with olive oil. Sprinkle with coarse salt, cumin and coriander seeds. Let rest for 5 minutes.

Using a pizza paddle or peel, transfer dough to the pizza stone and bake for 8 to 10 minutes, or until crisp and golden on bottom. Cool on wire rack.

MAKES 6 FLAT BREADS, SERVING 6

beef satay

In this appetizer I've borrowed from Indonesia and Thailand to create a spicy, tart, unforgettable satay. If you can't find the sambal oelek at the supermarket or an Asian grocery, just use any chile paste instead. For a twist, use this marinade in the flank steak recipe on page 106. It works like a dream.

1 large clove garlic, chopped	**SAUCE**
2 tbsp. tamarind paste (25 mL), soaked in warm water	juice of 1 lime
1 tbsp. sambal oelek (Indonesian chile sauce) (15 mL)	1 small Thai chile, finely chopped
1 tbsp. honey (15 mL)	1/4 cup smooth peanut butter (60 mL)
1 tsp. chopped fresh ginger (5 mL)	1/4 cup orange juice (60 mL)
1 tsp. hoisin sauce (5 mL)	2 tbsp. soy sauce (25 mL)
1/2 tsp. cumin seeds (2 mL), toasted and ground	1 tbsp. rice wine vinegar (15 mL)
1 lb. beef tenderloin or striploin (500 g)	1 tsp. grated fresh ginger (5 mL)
1/4 cup unsalted roasted peanuts (60 mL),	1 tsp. chopped fresh coriander, or to taste
chopped, for garnish	1 to 2 tbsp. water (15 to 25 mL)

In a blender, combine garlic, tamarind paste, sambal oelek, honey, ginger, hoisin sauce and cumin seeds. Process until smooth.

Slice beef across the grain into thin strips. Place beef in a glass dish or a resealable plastic bag. Add marinade and turn beef to coat. Marinate, refrigerated, for at least 2 hours, turning occasionally.

Preheat grill to high. Soak 8 to 10 bamboo skewers (6 inches/15 cm) in water for 20 minutes.

Meanwhile, make the sauce. Pulse all sauce ingredients in a food processor until smooth. Add a little water if sauce is too thick.

Remove beef from marinade (discarding marinade) and thread onto skewers. Grill (or broil) satays for 2 to 3 minutes per side or until cooked to desired doneness (cooking time will depend on thickness of meat). Serve satays with the sauce. Top with peanuts.

MAKES 8 TO 10 SKEWERS

swiss fondue

I was not a lover of fondue until I went to Switzerland and had the dish known as raclette. Raclette is made by melting the cheese of the same name and serving it with potatoes, bread and cornichons. It's ooey and gooey and delicious. I've transformed that memory into my own tangy smooth fondue. Though raclette is my favourite cheese to use in a fondue, because it's smooth and a little nutty, you can change the complexion of your own fondue by changing the cheese. Experiment with Gruyère, Swiss or Emmenthaler — just make sure you maintain the ratio of cheese to wine and cornstarch, to ensure the right consistency. Oh, and cornichons are small sour gherkins. Don't use sweet pickles!

14 small red new potatoes, scrubbed

1 large baguette

1 3/4 cups dry white wine (400 mL)

1 lb. Gruyère or raclette (500 g), shredded

1 1/2 tbsp. cornstarch (20 mL)

1/4 cup chopped fresh chives (60 mL)

freshly cracked black pepper to taste

3 or 4 cornichons per peson

Boil the potatoes until tender. Drain well, cut into bite-sized chunks if needed, and set aside. Cut the baguette into into bite-sized cubes; set aside.

In a large, heavy-bottomed saucepan, heat wine over medium heat until hot. Meanwhile, combine shredded cheese and cornstarch, mixing well with your hands until cheese is coated with cornstarch.

Add the cheese to hot wine in small batches, stirring with whisk after each addition and letting the cheese melt before adding the next batch. Continue until all cheese is used. With a wooden spoon, stir in the chives and pepper. Stir until smooth.

Transfer to a fondue pot and keep warm. Serve with the baguette cubes, boiled potatoes and cornichons.

SERVES 4

roasted squash and barley soup

When I first made this soup, I served it in baby pumpkins around Halloween. But I soon realized that no matter how I serve it, the rich, roasted flavour of the squash coupled with the crunch of the barley makes it simply irresistible. It's also a great way to introduce a nutritious hearty green — kale — into a recipe without it completely taking over. This soup is a main course in itself. Serve it with some bread and maybe a salad, and you have a comfy weeknight meal.

1/2 butternut squash, peeled and diced

1 tbsp. vegetable oil (15 mL)

pinch each ground cinnamon and freshly grated nutmeg

salt and freshly cracked black pepper to taste

2 tbsp. butter (25 mL)

1 large onion, chopped

2 cloves garlic, chopped

1 leek, washed well and chopped

1 carrot, diced

2 oz. pancetta or bacon (60 g), diced

1 cup pearl barley (250 mL)

2 bay leaves

5 sprigs fresh thyme

8 cups chicken stock (2 L)

several leaves kale, washed, chopped and steamed

Preheat oven to 375°F.

Spread diced squash in one layer on a large baking sheet. Drizzle with oil and season with cinnamon, nutmeg, salt and pepper. Roast squash, turning it once or twice so it cooks evenly, for 20 to 25 minutes, or until tender and golden.

Meanwhile, in a large skillet over medium heat, melt the butter. Cook onion, stirring frequently, until golden. Add the garlic, leek, carrot and pancetta; cook, stirring, another 2 to 3 minutes, or until garlic is golden. Stir in barley, bay leaves, thyme and stock. Bring to a boil, cover and reduce heat to low. Simmer, stirring occasionally, for about 30 minutes, or until barley is tender.

Add the roasted squash and simmer, uncovered, for 15 minutes. Adjust seasoning. Stir in kale and heat through. Discard bay leaves and thyme sprigs before serving.

SERVES 6

lentil and bacon soup

Here's a lentil soup that's a little bit smoky, a little bit tangy and a little bit spicy. It's a warming soup that is very satisfying, a super dish for a cool night — and the lentils are a great source of iron.

2 tbsp. olive oil (25 mL)

1 large onion, chopped

4 cloves garlic, sliced lengthwise

1 tsp. coriander seeds (5 mL), toasted and finely ground

1/2 tsp. cumin seeds (2 mL), toasted and finely ground

2 oz. pancetta (60 g), diced

1 dried small red chile, crushed, or chile flakes to taste

2 carrots, diced

2 stalks celery, diced

2 bay leaves

1/2 cup green lentils (125 mL)

1/2 cup red lentils (125 mL)

5 cups chicken stock (1.25 L)

salt and black pepper to taste

1 tbsp. sherry vinegar or red wine vinegar (15 mL)

In a large saucepan, heat the oil over medium heat. Cook onion, stirring frequently, until golden. Add garlic, coriander and cumin; cook, stirring, for 2 to 3 minutes, or until garlic is golden. Add pancetta, chile, carrots, celery, bay leaves, green lentils, red lentils, stock, salt and pepper. Bring to a boil, cover and reduce heat to low. Simmer for about 40 minutes, stirring occasionally. Uncover and simmer for 10 to 15 minutes, or until lentils are tender. Adjust seasoning and stir in the vinegar.

SERVES 4 TO 6

grilled wild mushroom soup

I've served this soup as a main course with a simple salad and some fresh bread, and you wouldn't believe how much everyone loves it. Grilling the mushrooms first makes this a mushroom soup unlike any other. The rice is an innovative way to thicken a soup without adding a ton of cream.

2 Portobello mushrooms, stems discarded	1/3 cup jasmine or basmati rice (75 mL)
4 shiitake mushrooms, stems discarded	1/3 cup dry sherry (75 mL)
1 tsp. vegetable oil (5 mL)	6 cups chicken or vegetable stock (1.5 L)
freshly cracked black pepper	3 sprigs fresh thyme
1 tbsp. butter (15 mL)	pinch grated nutmeg
4 shallots, chopped	salt and freshly cracked black pepper to taste
1 clove garlic, chopped	1/2 cup whipping (35%) cream (125 mL)
1 leek, white part only, washed well and chopped	2 tbsp. sour cream (25 mL)
2 stalks celery, diced	juice of 1/2 lemon
1/4 tsp. finely chopped fresh ginger (2 mL)	chopped fresh tarragon to taste, for garnish
4 cups assorted mushrooms (1 L), diced*	

Preheat grill to high.

Rub Portobello and shiitake mushrooms with oil; season with pepper. Grill mushrooms, top side down, for 4 to 5 minutes. Carefully remove mushrooms from grill, pouring into a small bowl any juices in the caps. Dice mushrooms and set aside.

In a large saucepan, melt butter over medium heat. Cook shallots, stirring, for 3 to 5 minutes, or until soft. Add the garlic, leek, celery and ginger. Continue to cook for 4 to 5 minutes, or until leeks are soft. Increase heat to high and add the fresh mushrooms, grilled mushrooms and reserved mushroom juice. Toss for 5 to 8 minutes over high heat until mushrooms are golden.

Stir in the rice, sherry, stock, thyme, nutmeg, salt and pepper. Bring to a boil, reduce heat to low and simmer, covered and stirring occasionally, for 30 minutes, or until vegetables are soft.

Stir in cream and simmer, uncovered, for 10 to 13 minutes, or until soup is thickened and rice is creamy. Discard the thyme sprigs. Stir in the sour cream, lemon juice and tarragon. Adjust the seasoning.

SERVES 4 TO 6

✳ The more flavour your mushrooms have, the better the soup will taste. I say, "Just say no to white button mushrooms." Use Portobello, oyster, shiitake, chanterelles, morels or any combination you like.

oven-roasted potato wedges with rosemary

Easy, easy, easy! Yummy, yummy, yummy! Simplicity is what sells these potatoes. The crisp golden texture of the potato sprinkled with the coarse salt will keep you craving more.

2 large red potatoes, scrubbed

leaves from 2 sprigs fresh rosemary, chopped

coarsely ground sea salt to taste

freshly cracked black pepper to taste

3 tbsp. olive oil (45 mL)

Preheat oven to 400°F. Lightly oil a baking sheet or line it with parchment paper.

Cut each potato into 8 wedges and transfer to a large bowl. Add the rosemary, salt, pepper and oil. Toss well until the potatoes are evenly coated.

Arrange potatoes in a single layer on baking sheet. Roast for 25 to 30 minutes, or until golden brown and crisp. Turn potatoes once or twice so they cook evenly, and remove any potatoes that brown sooner than the others.

SERVES 4

maui mashed potatoes

These potatoes will forever remind me of Maui, where I first had them. The recipe is unusual because it uses new potatoes, a real no-no for mashed potatoes. Roast the new potatoes in their skins and then mash them in the roasting pan with tons of sweet roasted garlic and herbs. I couldn't get enough of them the first time I ate them. Caution: heavy addiction factor!

6 medium red new potatoes, scrubbed

6 cloves garlic, peeled

2 tbsp. olive oil (25 mL)

salt and freshly cracked black pepper to taste

3 sprigs fresh thyme

1 sprig fresh rosemary

1/3 cup sour cream (75 mL)

1/3 cup whole milk (75 mL)

3 tbsp. butter (45 mL)

1 tbsp. chopped fresh parsley (15 mL)

1 tbsp. chopped fresh chives (15 mL)

pinch freshly grated nutmeg

Preheat oven to 375°F.

In a large roasting pan, toss potatoes and garlic in olive oil. Season with salt and plenty of pepper. Add thyme and rosemary sprigs. Roast for 40 to 45 minutes, or until potatoes are golden and tender, tossing occasionally to prevent scorching. Check garlic after about 25 minutes; if it is tender and golden, remove to prevent burning and return to the pan when potatoes have finished cooking.

Let potatoes cool for 10 minutes. Discard thyme and rosemary sprigs. Mash potatoes and garlic in the pan until potatoes are still a little chunky. Add the sour cream, milk, butter, parsley, chives and nutmeg; stir just to blend.

SERVES 6

smashed fried plantain

This method of twice frying plantain is very popular in parts of Latin America and yields a crispy golden slice that's soft in the middle. I always crave plantain when I eat something spicy.

Ripe plantain should be almost black outside for it to be soft enough inside. It shouldn't be eaten raw. To hasten ripening, place plantain in a paper bag on top of the fridge for a few days.

flour, for dredging
pinch ground allspice
2 ripe plantains
4 tbsp. vegetable oil (50 mL)
salt and freshly cracked black pepper to taste

In a small bowl, combine flour and allspice. Set aside.

Peel plantains and slice about 1/4 inch (5 mm) thick. In a large skillet over high heat, heat 2 tbsp. (25 mL) of the oil until hot. Fry plantain slices for about 2 minutes per side, or until golden. Drain on paper towels. Leave oil in the skillet.

Line a cutting board with parchment paper. Transfer plantain to cutting board and cover with another piece of parchment. Smash each slice with a skillet or mallet until flat. Lightly dredge slices in flavoured flour.

Return skillet to high heat and add remaining 2 tbsp. (25 mL) oil; heat until almost smoking. Fry plantain a second time until golden on both sides, 1 to 2 minutes.

Sprinkle with salt and freshly cracked black pepper.

SERVES 4

great greek baked beans

This is my dad's secret (until now) way of making beans. I have perfected his recipe (I'd never tell him, though). They are great warm, at room temperature, as an accompaniment or just as part of an appetizer platter.

2 cups dried lima beans or white kidney beans (500 mL)

2 tbsp. extra virgin olive oil (25 mL)

1 large onion, chopped

4 cloves garlic, sliced lengthwise

3 stalks celery, diced

4 carrots, diced

several sprigs fresh thyme

2 bay leaves

big pinch dried oregano (preferably Greek)

1/2 small dried chile pepper, crushed

1 can (28 oz./796 mL) diced tomatoes with juice

1 cup water (250 mL)

2 tbsp. honey (25 mL)

salt and freshly cracked black pepper to taste

Soak beans in enough water to cover for 4 hours. Drain beans and transfer to a large saucepan. Cover with cold water and bring to a boil over high heat. Reduce heat to low and simmer, uncovered, for 30 to 35 minutes, or until beans are just tender. Drain.

Meanwhile, heat oil in a large skillet over high heat. Sauté onion and garlic for 4 to 5 minutes, or until golden. Stir in celery, carrots, thyme, bay leaves, oregano, chile, tomatoes, water, honey, salt and pepper. Bring to a boil, reduce heat to low and simmer, covered, for 1 hour, or until sauce has thickened slightly and vegetables are tender.

Meanwhile, preheat oven to 375°F.

Combine sauce and beans in a medium baking dish and bake, uncovered, for 20 to 25 minutes, or until mixture is thick and bubbly. Discard thyme sprigs and bay leaves before serving.

SERVES 8

gooey baked mac and three cheeses

There is no way you'll get me to make or eat mac and cheese from a package. This is my totally irresistible way of making this classic favourite. The real Mac-Coy! Any kind of short pasta will work, but on the cheese side, I am extremist. I had to use three different cheeses, but you don't have to. Any sharp cheese along with a smoother one will give you great homemade flavour and texture. Come to think of it, goat cheese wouldn't be a bad addition. I wonder if I have any in the fridge right now?

1 lb. macaroni or any short pasta such as rotini, fusilli or shells (500 g)

1/4 cup butter (60 mL)

1/4 cup all-purpose flour (60 mL)

3 cups milk (750 mL)

1 tbsp. chopped fresh thyme (15 mL)

big pinch freshly grated nutmeg

pinch cayenne

salt and black pepper to taste

3/4 cup shredded good-quality old cheddar (175 mL)

3/4 cup shredded fontina (175 mL)

1/4 cup grated Grana Padano or Parmigiano-Reggiano (60 mL) (optional)

Cook macaroni in a large pot of boiling salted water until al dente. Drain well.

Meanwhile, in a medium saucepan over medium heat, melt butter. Add the flour and stir with wooden spoon until a paste forms. Remove from heat and add the cold milk a little at a time, stirring well between each addition so you have a smooth sauce. Return pot to heat and cook, stirring constantly, until sauce comes to a boil and thickens. Stir in thyme, nutmeg, cayenne, salt and pepper. Remove from heat and add the cheddar and fontina. Stir until cheese melts.

Preheat broiler. Brush an 8- by 10-inch baking dish with melted butter.

Add macaroni to cheese sauce and stir to mix well. Transfer to baking dish. Sprinkle with Grana Padano if desired. Place under broiler until browned and bubbly, 3 to 4 minutes.

SERVES 4 TO 6

bolognese lasagna

After having tasted this lasagna in the city of Bologna, in Italy, I have made it official that I can't eat lasagna any other way. It's the perfect balance of cream, cheese and meat. The layers of pasta are ultra thin (if you feel like making your own pasta) and the béchamel sauce gives it a creamy texture without being heavy. A true Bolognese meat sauce is made with milk, but because the béchamel has plenty of milk in it already, I'm fearless enough to make the executive decision to omit it. Although fresh noodles are readily available in most grocery stores, you can also use dried lasagna noodles; just cook them until al dente.

MEAT SAUCE

3 tbsp. olive oil (45 mL)

2 onions, finely chopped

1 1/2 lb. lean ground beef (750 g)

1 small spicy Italian sausage, casing removed

2 cloves garlic, chopped

2 small carrots, finely diced

1 can (28 oz./796 mL) plum tomatoes with juice, chopped

several sprigs fresh thyme

couple bay leaves

1 to 2 tsp. dried oregano (5 to 10 mL)

salt and freshly cracked black pepper to taste

leaves from 1 bunch fresh basil, chopped

BÉCHAMEL SAUCE

1/3 cup butter (75 mL)

1/3 cup all-purpose flour (75 mL)

4 cups milk (1 L)

pinch freshly grated nutmeg

salt and black pepper to taste

1/3 cup freshly grated Parmigiano-Reggiano and/or pecorino cheese (75 mL)

12 oz. fresh lasagna noodles (375 g)

salt and freshly cracked black pepper to taste

To make the meat sauce, in a large skillet, heat the olive oil over medium heat. Add the onions and cook, stirring frequently, for 3 to 4 minutes, or until soft. Add the ground beef and sausage; cook, stirring frequently, for 5 to 7 minutes, or until browned. Add the garlic and carrots and cook for 3 minutes just to soften.

Add the tomatoes, thyme, bay leaves, oregano, salt and pepper. Bring to a boil, reduce heat to low and simmer, covered and stirring occasionally, for 55 to 60 minutes, or until sauce is thickened and flavour has developed to your liking. Discard the thyme sprigs and bay leaves. Stir in the fresh basil and adjust seasoning. Set aside.

To make the béchamel sauce, in a medium saucepan over medium heat, melt butter. Add the flour and stir with a wooden spoon until a paste forms. Remove from heat and add the cold milk a little at a time, stirring well between each addition so you have a smooth sauce. Return pot to heat and cook, stirring constantly, until sauce comes to a boil and thickens. Stir in nutmeg, salt and pepper to taste. Add some of the pecorino and Parmesan cheese and stir.

Preheat oven to 350°F. Oil the bottom of a 13- by 9-inch baking dish.

Cook pasta in a large pot of boiling salted water for 4 minutes, or until just al dente. Transfer to bowl with cold water to prevent sticking. Drain on a kitchen towel.

Spread several spoonfuls of meat sauce in the baking dish. Cover with a layer of noodles. Add one third of the meat sauce, one third of the cheese and one quarter of the béchamel. Continue to layer, ending with béchamel. Sprinkle with remaining cheese.

Bake lasagna in middle of oven for 35 to 40 minutes, or until golden and bubbling. Let sit for about 10 minutes before cutting into it so that the layers set and don't ooze too much when you serve.

SERVES 6 TO 8

flaky potato and brie tart

Potatoes, Brie and pancetta wrapped in a flaky crust. Do I really need to say anything more? Irresistible!

PASTRY

1 cup all-purpose flour (250 mL)

1/3 cup cold butter (75 mL)

1/2 tsp. salt (2 mL)

1/4 tsp. cracked black pepper (1 mL)

1 egg yolk

1/4 cup buttermilk (60 mL)

FILLING

1 large Yukon Gold potato

1 cup half-and-half (10%) cream (250 mL)

salt and freshly cracked black pepper to taste

1 tbsp. butter (15 mL)

3 large shallots, thinly sliced

1 tbsp. chopped fresh thyme (15 mL)

1 oz. pancetta or bacon (30 g), chopped

1 large egg yolk

1/4 cup chopped fresh parsley (60 mL)

pinch cayenne

freshly grated nutmeg to taste

3 oz. Brie (90 g), cut into small pieces

sprigs fresh thyme

To make the pastry, in a food processor, combine the flour, butter, salt and pepper. Pulse until mixture resembles coarse meal. Do not overwork or pastry will be tough.

In a medium bowl, whisk together egg yolk and buttermilk. Add the flour mixture and work gently with your hands just until dough comes together. Turn onto a lightly floured surface and knead very gently to combine. Flatten into a disk and wrap with plastic. Chill for 30 minutes.

Preheat oven to 375°F.

On a lightly floured surface, roll pastry out into a circle 11 inches (25 cm) wide and 1/8 inch (3 mm) thick. Transfer to a 9-inch (23 cm) fluted flan ring and press down gently. With a rolling pin, roll over the pan to cut off the excess pastry. Prick holes in the bottom of pastry with fork and freeze for 10 minutes. Line pastry with foil and fill with dried beans or pie weights.

Bake pastry on the bottom rack for 25 to 30 minutes, or until pastry begins to crisp on the sides. Remove foil with beans and cook pastry for 15 more minutes, or until crisp and golden. Let cool slightly.

Reduce heat to 325°F.

Meanwhile, make the filling. Peel and thinly slice the potato. In a small saucepan, cover sliced potatoes with cream. Season with salt and pepper. Bring to a boil over high heat, reduce heat to low and simmer, covered, until potatoes are just tender. With a slotted spoon transfer potatoes to a plate to cool. Reserve cream.

In a medium skillet, melt butter over low heat. Cook shallots and chopped thyme, stirring occasionally, for 10 to 12 minutes, or until very soft and golden. Add the pancetta and cook until lightly browned, 3 to 5 minutes. Remove from heat.

In a small bowl, whisk together the reserved cream, the yolk, parsley, cayenne and nutmeg. Season with salt and pepper.

Spread shallots and pancetta over pastry. Arrange potato slices in a single layer over shallots, overlapping slightly if necessary. Pour cream mixture over potato slices. Arrange the Brie evenly on top. Decorate with thyme sprigs and bake until filling sets and is golden, about 20 minutes.

SERVES 8

calzone bursting with spinach and buffalo mozzarella

Whenever I make this stuffed pizza with creamy buffalo mozzarella and spicy chorizo sausage, I have to forbid myself seconds or I'll just keep eating and finish the whole tray. Make sure you poke a hole in the middle for steam to escape or the calzone gets soggy. I also bake it at a super-hot temperature to maintain that crispy crust. If you choose, you can even make it as a pizza.

DOUGH

1 pkg. active dry yeast

3/4 cup lukewarm water (175 mL)

2 cups all-purpose flour (500 mL)

1 tsp. salt (5 mL)

1/4 cup olive oil (60 mL)

FILLING

2 tbsp. olive oil (25 mL)

1 onion, chopped

1/4 lb. chorizo sausage (125 g), casing removed

1 bunch fresh spinach, blanched

4 green onions, finely chopped

6 Italian black olives, pitted and quartered

pinch freshly grated nutmeg

freshly cracked black pepper to taste

4 oz. buffalo mozzarella (125 g), cut into chunks

3 oz. firm goat cheese (90 g), crumbled

1 egg, whisked with 1 tbsp. (15 mL) water

To make the dough, in a small bowl, whisk yeast into warm water. Let stand for 10 minutes or until foamy. In a food processor fitted with the dough blade, combine the flour and salt. Add the oil to the yeast mixture. Pour liquid into flour and pulse until mixture comes together. Keep pulsing until dough is almost smooth.

Turn dough onto a lightly floured surface. Knead dough until smooth. If dough is too sticky, dust with more flour. Place in a well-oiled bowl and cover with plastic wrap. Let rise in warm spot until doubled in size, about 1 1/2 hours.

Punch down dough and divide into 6 equal pieces. Roll loosely into balls and sprinkle with flour. Cover with a tea towel and let rest for 30 minutes.

Meanwhile, make the filling. Heat oil in a large skillet over medium heat. Cook onion, stirring frequently, for 2 to 3 minutes, or until soft. Add chorizo and cook for 3 to 4 minutes, or until sausage is just golden. Remove from heat.

Squeeze excess moisture out of blanched spinach and chop coarsely. Stir spinach, green onions and olives into sausage mixture. Season with nutmeg and pepper. Spread on a baking sheet to cool completely. When the mixture has cooled, stir in mozzarella and goat cheese. Add salt if necessary.

Preheat oven to 450°F. Line a baking sheet with parchment paper.

On a lightly floured surface, roll each ball of dough into a 6-inch (15 cm) disk. Brush edges with eggwash. Divide the filling between the 6 rounds, mounding it on the bottom half of each round and leaving a 1/2-inch (1 cm) border. Fold top of round over and seal edges by pressing with a fork.

With a small knife, cut a small hole in the top of each calzone. Transfer calzones to the baking sheet and brush with eggwash. Let the calzones rest for 10 minutes before baking.

Bake for 13 to 15 minutes, or until golden and puffed. Cool on wire racks for at least 15 minutes before serving. You can also bake them on a pizza stone.

SERVES 6

grilled grouper with crisp fennel salad and lemon spiced pilaf

I think grouper is so underrated. It's in the sea bass family, but it's not quite as rich. This quick grill shows off grouper's firm but tender and delicious flesh. Grouper with this Crisp Fennel Salad is a brilliant marriage. Add the Lemon Spiced Pilaf and take the dish to another stratosphere!

GRILLED GROUPER

2 tbsp. olive oil (25 mL)

1 tbsp. chopped fresh parsley (15 mL)

1 tbsp. chopped fresh thyme (15 mL)

1 tbsp. chopped fresh coriander (15 mL)

1/2 tsp. cumin seeds (2 mL), toasted and ground

grated zest of 2 lemons

4 grouper fillets, skin on (each 6 oz./175 g)

salt and cracked black pepper to taste

Preheat grill to high.

In a small bowl, stir together the oil, parsley, thyme, coriander, cumin seeds and lemon zest. Rub mixture on top of the grouper. Season with salt and pepper. Grill grouper, flesh side down, for 4 minutes. Turn fish over and grill for another 4 minutes, or until cooked through.

CRISP FENNEL SALAD

2 tbsp. olive oil (25 mL)

2 tbsp. Champagne vinegar, sherry vinegar or apple cider vinegar (25 mL)

1/2 tsp. coarse salt (2 mL)

1/4 cup chopped fresh parsley (60 mL)

1/2 small red onion, thinly sliced

1/2 bulb fennel, very thinly sliced (preferably with a mandoline)

grated zest of 1 lemon

freshly cracked black pepper to taste

pinch sugar

Combine all ingredients in a medium bowl and toss well.

LEMON SPICED PILAF

1 cup basmati rice (250 mL), rinsed

1 3/4 cups chicken stock (425 mL)

1 tbsp. olive oil (15 mL)

1 tsp. cumin seeds (5 mL), toasted and ground

1/4 tsp. ground sumac (1 mL) or juice of 1/2 lemon

1 small red pepper, cubed

1 cinnamon stick

grated zest of 1 lemon

salt and black pepper to taste

Combine all ingredients in a large, heavy-bottomed saucepan. Bring to a boil and reduce heat to low. Cover and simmer for 12 minutes. Do not remove lid. Remove from heat and let stand for 5 minutes. Fluff rice with a fork.

Serve grouper over or under the fennel salad, with the rice on the side.

SERVES 4

thai-spiced chicken drumsticks

If it's a drumstick, usually everyone will try it. This is where I sneak in some creativity by dressing the chicken in Thai clothing. If you are cooking for kids, these are a touch spicy, so you may want to reduce the chile.

2 cloves garlic, finely chopped

2 Thai chiles, finely chopped

1/4 cup fish sauce (60 mL)

2 tbsp. grated fresh ginger (25 mL)

2 tbsp. sesame oil (25 mL)

1 1/2 tbsp. honey (20 mL)

1 tbsp. soy sauce (15 mL)

1 tsp. coriander seeds (5 mL), toasted and ground

1 tsp. cumin seeds (5 mL), toasted and ground

salt and black pepper to taste

12 chicken drumsticks

Preheat oven to 375°F.

In a large bowl, combine garlic, chiles, fish sauce, ginger, sesame oil, honey, soy sauce, coriander seeds, cumin seeds, salt and pepper. Add drumsticks and toss to coat well.

Arrange in a single layer on a baking sheet or shallow baking pan. Bake for 30 to 35 minutes, or until chicken is cooked through and golden brown.

SERVES 4 TO 6

crispy lemon roasted chicken

Every time I make chicken for my mom, this is the one she goes crazy over. She loves lots of tang too! She especially likes the ton of lemons as well as the super-crispy skin. If she had it her way, she'd steal everyone else's chicken skin right off their plates.

2 1/2 lemons

1 small grain-fed roasting chicken (2 1/2 lb./1.25 kg)

several sprigs each fresh rosemary and thyme

2 small onions, peeled and quartered

6 cloves garlic

2 tbsp. olive oil (25 mL)

leaves from several sprigs each fresh rosemary and thyme, chopped

1 tsp. paprika (5 mL)

coarse salt and freshly cracked black pepper to taste

Preheat oven to 400°F.

Cut 2 lemons into 4 wedges each. Juice the remaining 1/2 lemon. Fill the chicken cavity with the rosemary and thyme sprigs, half the lemon wedges, 1 of the onions, 2 cloves of the garlic, salt and pepper. Truss the bird, if desired. (If you don't want to fuss, that's fine, I won't tell. It'll still taste great.) Rub chicken all over with the lemon juice. Drizzle with olive oil and sprinkle with chopped rosemary and thyme, paprika, salt and pepper.

Lay chicken on a rack in a small roasting pan. Arrange remaining lemon wedges, onion and garlic around chicken. Roast, without basting, for 40 minutes. Reduce heat to 375°F and roast, without basting, for 20 to 25 minutes, or until juices run clear. Let chicken rest for about 15 minutes before carving.

If you want to use the pan dripping to serve with the chicken, spoon off most of the fat. Set the pan over high heat and deglaze with a splash of wine (if desired) and 3/4 cup (175 mL) chicken stock. Cook, scraping up all the sticky bits in the pan (this is what adds loads of flavour), until reduced by about half.

SERVES 4

french-canadian shepherd's pie

I adore the homey flavours of tourtière, but sometimes I find the pastry makes it a little too heavy. So I came up with this combination of the lightness of a shepherd's pie with the depth of a tourtière. You can use all ground pork or all turkey if you don't feel like combining the two.

TOPPING

2 small sweet potatoes, peeled and quartered

2 medium Yukon Gold potatoes, peeled and quartered

1/2 cup half-and-half (10%) cream (125 mL)

1 tbsp. butter (15 mL)

pinch ground allspice

freshly grated nutmeg to taste

salt and freshly cracked black pepper to taste

chopped fresh chives to taste

FILLING

1 tbsp. butter (15 mL)

1 lb. ground pork (500 g)

1/2 lb. ground turkey (250 g)

4 large shallots, finely chopped

2 cloves garlic, chopped

2 stalks celery, finely diced

2 carrots, finely diced

2 tsp. chopped fresh thyme (10 mL)

1/2 tsp. dried savory (2 mL)

1/2 tsp. chopped fresh rosemary (2 mL)

1/4 tsp. ground allspice (1 mL)

1/2 tsp. cinnamon (2 mL)

2 tsp. Worcestershire sauce (10 mL)

1 tbsp. Dijon mustard (15 mL)

1/2 cup chicken stock (125 mL)

salt and pepper to taste

3/4 cup fresh or frozen green peas (175 mL)

Preheat oven to 375°F. Line a roasting pan with foil or parchment paper.

To make the topping, place potatoes in a pot of salted cold water. Bring to a boil, reduce heat and simmer for 15 to 20 minutes, or until fork-tender. Drain well. Rice potatoes into a bowl (or mash). Add cream and butter; mash again. Season with allspice, nutmeg, salt, pepper and chives. Mash until well mixed.

To make the filling, in a large, deep skillet, melt the butter over high heat. Sauté the pork, turkey, shallots and garlic until meat is golden, 4 to 5 minutes. Add the celery, carrots, thyme, savory, rosemary, all-spice and cinnamon. Cook, stirring frequently, until carrots begin to soften, about 4 minutes. Add the Worcestershire sauce, mustard and stock. Bring to a boil and reduce heat to low. Season with salt and pepper. Cover and simmer for about 20 minutes, or until meat is tender and moisture is absorbed. Remove from heat and stir in the peas.

Transfer filling to a medium rectangular baking dish at least 2 inches (5 cm) deep. Top with potato mixture, spreading it to completely cover meat. Bake at 375°F for 15 to 20 minutes, or until top is golden.

SERVES 6 TO 8

apple chile bbq baby back ribs

These ribs are great for any season. They are slightly sweet, spicy and smoky. I love poaching my ribs first until they almost fall off the bone. Then they will suck in all that intense sauce while they are still warm. Finally, off they go for a few minutes on the grill to deepen their colour.

2 lb. baby back pork ribs (1 kg)	1/3 cup tomato juice (75 mL)
1 tsp. mustard seeds (5 mL)	1/4 cup apple juice (60 mL)
2 cloves garlic, crushed	3 tbsp. ketchup (45 mL)
1 onion, sliced	2 tbsp. apple butter (25 mL)
1/2 dried chile, crushed	2 tbsp. balsamic vinegar (25 mL)
8 whole cloves	1 tbsp. soy sauce (15 mL)
4 allspice berries	1 tsp. paprika (5 mL)
freshly cracked black pepper to taste	1 tsp. Worcestershire sauce (5 mL)
1 large clove garlic, finely chopped	1 tsp. honey (5 mL)
1 small chipotle chile,	1 tsp. Dijon mustard (5 mL)
soaked in hot water and finely chopped*	salt to taste

Place ribs in large pot and cover with cold water. Add mustard seeds, garlic, onion, chile, cloves, allspice and black pepper. Bring to a boil. Skim off the froth, reduce heat to low and simmer, covered, for 70 to 80 minutes, or until meat is tender. Drain ribs.

In a small bowl, stir together the garlic, chipotle chile, tomato juice, apple juice, ketchup, apple butter, vinegar, soy sauce, paprika, Worcestershire sauce, honey, mustard and salt. Place ribs in a roasting pan and cover with the apple juice mixture. Let sit for 5 minutes, turning every few minutes to coat well.

Preheat grill to high and brush rack well with oil.

Reduce grill to medium. Remove ribs from apple juice mixture, reserving mixture. Grill ribs, basting frequently with apple juice mixture, for 3 to 5 minutes on each side or until browned. Do not let the ribs dry out while grilling them. If flames get too high, move the ribs away from direct flames.

In a small saucepan over high heat, boil any remaining apple mixture for a few minutes to cook out any raw meat juices. Pour over ribs.

SERVES 4 TO 6

✱ Chipotle chiles are fairly hot. If you're worried, start by adding only half a chile. Taste the marinade and add a little more to your liking.

jamaican ribs

These ribs feature a combination of jerk seasoning and BBQ sauce. The power of the scotch bonnets, fresh thyme and allspice slaps you right in the face. Sometimes that can be good thing if you are daring! Dried herbs just don't work here because you really want the earthy flavour of the thyme leaves to balance the sweet allspice berries, not to mention the killer chiles.

2 lb. baby back pork ribs (1 kg)

2 cloves garlic, crushed

2 stalks celery, chopped

1 onion, sliced

1 scotch bonnet chile

8 whole cloves

6 allspice berries

BASTING SAUCE

juice of 2 limes

juice of 2 oranges

leaves from 1 large bunch fresh thyme, finely chopped

1 1/2 scotch bonnet chiles, minced

6 cloves garlic, finely chopped

4 green onions, minced

6 tbsp. brown sugar (90 mL)

6 tbsp. ketchup (90 mL)

2 tbsp. Worcestershire sauce (25 mL)

1 tsp. ground allspice (5 mL)

1/2 tsp. cinnamon (2 mL)

salt to taste

Place ribs in a large pot and cover with cold water. Add garlic, celery, onion, chile, cloves and allspice. Bring to a boil. Skim, reduce heat to low and simmer, covered, for 1 hour, or until meat is tender. Drain and keep warm.

Meanwhile, preheat oven to 375°F.

Combine the basting sauce ingredients.

Place warm ribs in a roasting pan and cover with 3/4 of the basting sauce, saving the rest for basting. Bake ribs for 20 minutes, turning and basting ribs frequently so they are evenly browned and coated with sauce.

SERVES 4 TO 6

chimichurri-seared rib-eye steak with chipotle beans

Chimichurri is one of those food words I love to say. It's a condiment from Argentina that I have given my own twist to. The beans provide a round full backdrop for the tart and slightly pungent chimichurri beef. It's the absolute best on the BBQ!

CHIPOTLE BEANS

2 tbsp. vegetable oil (25 mL)

1 large onion, diced

2 sprigs fresh thyme

1 bay leaf

4 cloves garlic, chopped

1 can (28 oz./796 mL) plum tomatoes, diced, with juice

1 cup water (250 mL)

1 carrot, diced

1 small dried chipotle chile

1 small cinnamon stick

1 tbsp. brown sugar (15 mL)

1 tbsp. molasses (15 mL)

1/4 tsp. cumin seeds (1 mL), ground

salt and black pepper to taste

1 can (14 oz./398 mL) pinto beans, drained and rinsed

chopped fresh coriander, for garnish

In a medium saucepan over high heat, heat the oil. Sauté onion 5 minutes, or until soft. Add thyme, bay leaf and garlic. Sauté 3 to 4 minutes, or until garlic is soft. Add the tomatoes, water, carrot, chipotle chile, cinnamon, sugar, molasses, cumin and salt and pepper. Bring to a boil, reduce heat to low and simmer, uncovered and stirring occasionally, for 20 minutes. Stir in the beans and simmer for 15 to 20 minutes, or until sauce thickens. Discard thyme sprigs and bay leaf. Set aside and keep warm.

CHIMICHURRI-SEARED RIB-EYE STEAK

grated zest of 1 lemon

2 cloves garlic, chopped

3 tbsp. roughly chopped fresh parsley (45 mL)

2 tbsp. roughly chopped fresh coriander (25 mL)

1 tsp. dried oregano (5 mL)

2 tbsp. extra virgin olive oil (25 mL)

2 small rib-eye steaks (each 8 oz./250 g)

salt and cracked black pepper to taste

Preheat grill to high.

In a food processor, combine lemon zest, garlic, parsley, coriander and oregano; pulse until well combined. Add the olive oil and pulse until smooth. Rub both sides of steaks with chimichurri and season with salt and pepper. Grill for 4 to 5 minutes per side for medium-rare or until done to your liking. Let steaks rest for 10 minutes before slicing.

Slice steaks across the grain and serve with the chipotle beans. Garnish chipotle beans with coriander.

SERVES 4

chicken tacos with picante papaya mojo

No store-bought tacos will ever hold a candle to these delicious, spicy, smoky tacos topped with brightly coloured mojo. They require a bit of prep, and I insist on the highest quality ingredients — but otherwise they're a snap.

2 boneless skinless chicken breasts

1/2 small chipotle chili soaked in hot water,
   finely chopped

1/2 tsp. cumin seeds, crushed (2 mL)

2 tbsp. chopped fresh coriander (30 mL)

salt and freshly cracked black pepper to taste

2 tsp. vegetable oil (10 mL)

4 taco shells

PAPAYA MOJO

1 small ripe papaya, peeled, seeded and diced

1 small red onion, finely chopped

1 clove garlic, minced

juice of half a lime

2 tbsp. chopped fresh parsley (30 mL)

1/2 tsp. chopped fresh jalapeno (2 mL)

1/4 tsp. salt (1 mL)

shredded lettuce, sour cream and diced avocado, for garnish

Preheat oven to 375° F.

Rub chicken breasts with the chipotle chili, cumin seeds, coriander and salt and pepper.

Heat oil in a skillet over high heat. When oil is hot, sear the chicken for about 3 minutes on each side, or until golden. Transfer chicken to a roasting pan and bake for 8 to 10 minutes, or until juices run clear. While the chicken is baking, place taco shells on a baking sheet and toast them in the oven for 5 minutes. Remove chicken and tacos from the oven. When chicken has cooled, dice into small chunks and set aside.

To make the papaya mojo, combine half the mojo ingredients in a blender and pulse until smooth. Combine with remaining half in a small bowl. Cover and chill until ready to use. Adjust seasoning before serving.

To assemble, fill taco shells with chicken chunks and top with papaja mojo, lettuce, sour cream and avocado.

SERVES 2 OR 4

In this chapter we take a walk on the wild side. These recipes are out of the ordinary, present some technical challeng or use unusual ingredients. Here is your chance to be ultra-fearless in the kitchen. There are many daring recipes to conqu in this chapter: Dark Ale–Battered Halibut and Chips Grilled Pizza with Arugula, Peppers and Niçoise Olive and Moroccan Chicken Pie.

radicchio di treviso and jerusalem artichoke salad

This recipe is daring not because it's complicated to execute but because the fresh Jerusalem artichoke is available only in fall and winter. The radicchio di Treviso (it's the long, whiter radicchio, not the round one) is also a little harder to find, but it is much less bitter than round radicchio and definitely worth the search. If I can find it, I always choose the Treviso variety. It is named for the region near Venice from where it originates.

4 medium Jerusalem artichokes, peeled and cut in half
2 tbsp. olive oil (25 mL)
salt and freshly cracked black pepper
1 head radicchio di Treviso, leaves pulled apart and washed

DRESSING
1 small clove garlic, finely minced
juice of 1/2 lemon
1/3 cup extra virgin olive oil (75 mL)
1/4 cup chopped fresh parsley (60 mL)
1/4 cup sherry vinegar (60 mL)
salt and freshly cracked black pepper to taste

Preheat oven to 375°F.

Toss the Jerusalem artichokes in olive oil and season with salt and pepper. Roast in a small roasting pan for 15 to 20 minutes, or until tender. Set aside.

Trim radicchio and arrange leaves on a platter. Arrange artichoke halves on top of the radicchio, spreading them out evenly.

Combine the dressing ingredients in a small bowl and whisk until blended. Drizzle over salad.

SERVES 4

artichokes in lemon chive beurre blanc

If just reading the words "beurre blanc" makes you think about ordering in, relax. It's just a technical French phrase for white butter sauce that is based on simple technique. I throw in the artichoke for even more fun. My advice is to make sure the butter is cold and cut into small bits, and to add it very slowly to the sauce or the sauce won't thicken. It takes only a few minutes to get a smooth creamy sauce, but beurre blanc waits for no one, so plan on steaming the artichokes first, so you can concentrate on the sauce at the end for perfect timing. Feel free to use this sauce with asparagus, green beans, even broccoli. So don't just butter your vegetables – beurre blanc them!

4 large artichokes, stems trimmed

juice of 1 lemon

LEMON CHIVE BEURRE BLANC

2 shallots, very finely chopped

3 tbsp. dry white wine (45 mL)

2 tbsp. white wine vinegar (25 mL)

1 tbsp. lemon juice (15 mL)

1/2 cup cold butter (125 mL), cut into small cubes

1 tbsp. chopped fresh chives (15 mL)

1 tsp. grated lemon zest (5 mL)

salt and freshly cracked black pepper to taste

Cut about 1 inch (2.5 cm) from the top of each artichoke and pull off any browned outer leaves. Place stem down in a saucepan just large enough to hold them. Add enough water to cover artichokes. Squeeze the lemon juice over top. Cover and bring to a boil. Reduce heat and simmer until artichokes are tender, about 20 minutes. Remove from water and let cool.

To make the beurre blanc, stir together the shallots, wine, vinegar and lemon juice in a medium nonreactive saucepan. Boil on high heat, without stirring, until reduced to 1 tbsp. (15 mL). Reduce heat to very low and begin whisking in the cold butter a little at a time. Keep watching the butter to ensure that it is blending in with sauce but not melting; if it is melting too quickly, remove saucepan from heat and whisk off heat for a minute or so.

When all the butter is incorporated, remove from heat and stir in the chives, lemon zest, salt and pepper.

Transfer beurre blanc to small dipping bowls and serve with artichokes.

SERVES 4

basteeya (moroccan chicken pie)

Please don't run away. Just because you maybe can't pronounce it doesn't mean you can't cook it. This is a killer Moroccan crisp phyllo pie. The combination of cinnamon, icing sugar and almonds hidden between the layers of phyllo and the sweet and savoury chicken filling is delicious. It has a lot of ingredients, but they are essential to create that delicate balance of sweet and salty. This dish doesn't offer too much room for improvisation, but the flavours are definitely daring!

2 tbsp. olive oil (25 mL)

1 large onion, chopped

2 cloves garlic, chopped

1 small Thai chile, chopped, or 1/2 tsp. chile flakes (2 mL)

1 cinnamon stick

1 tsp. good-quality Madras curry powder (5 mL)

1 tsp. chopped fresh ginger (5 mL)

1 tsp. grated lemon zest (5 mL)

4 cooked chicken legs, boned and meat cut in chunks

2 pitted prunes, chopped

1/4 cup spicy green olives (60 mL), pitted and diced

1/2 cup chicken stock (125 mL)

juice of 1/2 lemon

salt and cracked black pepper to taste

2 tbsp. whole toasted almonds (25 mL)

1 tbsp. icing sugar (15 mL)

1/2 tsp. ground cinnamon (2 mL)

1/3 cup melted butter or olive oil (75 mL)

8 sheets phyllo

1 egg, lightly beaten

2 tbsp. chopped fresh coriander (25 mL)

In a large skillet, heat olive oil over medium-high heat. Sauté the onion until soft, about 5 minutes. Add the garlic, chile, cinnamon stick, curry powder, ginger, lemon zest and chicken; sauté for 2 minutes. Stir in prunes, olives, stock, lemon juice, salt and pepper. Bring to a boil. Reduce heat to low, cover and simmer, without stirring, for 10 minutes. Remove lid and simmer for a further 5 minutes, or until liquid has evaporated. Let cool completely.

Meanwhile, pulse almonds, icing sugar and cinnamon in a food processor until coarsely chopped.

Preheat oven to 375°F. Brush a 10-inch (25 cm) pie dish with some of the melted butter.

On a work surface, arrange a sheet of phyllo; keep remaining phyllo under a damp tea towel. Brush phyllo with melted butter. Lay in the middle of pie dish, allowing excess phyllo to hang over edge. Repeat with 4 more sheets of phyllo.

Stir beaten egg and coriander into chicken mixture. Spoon chicken mixture into pie dish. Fold the overhanging phyllo pieces into the middle of the pie, sprinkling some of the almond mixture between each layer.

Butter 1 remaining piece of phyllo, and sprinkle with some almond mixture. Place over filling and tuck in any overhang. Repeat with remaining phyllo and almond mixture. (Do these one by one, not stacked together, to achieve a light, blossomy top.)

Bake for 20 minutes, or until top is browned and crisp. Let stand for 5 minutes before cutting into wedges.

SERVES 6

grilled pizza with arugula, peppers and niçoise olives

Grilling pizza gives the crust a crisp, smoky exterior that is hard to achieve in an oven, unless you're lucky enough to have a wood-burning one. Once you put the dough on the grill, you have to keep an eye on it or it will soon be charcoal. I get all my toppings ready next to the grill before I start. As soon as the crust is crisp on one side, I flip it over and slap on my toppings. Again, we're talking process and not recipe. You can use any combination of toppings as long as they're not moist — you don't want to ruin that crisp crust.

DOUGH

3/4 cup lukewarm water (175 mL)

1 tbsp. sugar (15 mL)

1/2 pkg. active dry yeast

1 cup all-purpose flour (250 mL)

1/2 cup corn flour (125 mL)

3/4 tsp. salt (4 mL)

2 tbsp. olive oil (25 mL)

TOPPING

2 tbsp. extra virgin olive oil (25 mL)

a few niçoise olives, pitted and cut in half

1 roasted red pepper, cut into strips

1 red onion, sliced

1 head garlic, roasted and squeezed out of skin*

5 to 6 leaves arugula, torn

4 oz. buffalo mozzarella (125 g), thinly sliced

In a small bowl, stir together the water and sugar. Whisk in yeast. Let stand until slightly foamy, about 5 minutes. In a food processor fitted with dough blade, combine the all-purpose flour, corn flour and salt. Add yeast mixture and pulse several times. Add oil and pulse again. Dough will be very sticky at this point. Turn dough onto a well-floured surface and knead by hand until smooth and elastic, about 5 minutes. The dough should be soft but not sticky. If dough is too sticky, add a little more flour. Place dough in a lightly oiled medium bowl and cover. Let rest in a warm spot until doubled, about 1 1/2 hours.

Punch down dough, cover and let rest again for 30 minutes. Divide dough into 2 equal balls. Cover and let rest again for 10 minutes.

Preheat grill to high. Lightly oil a baking sheet. Line a second baking sheet with parchment paper and sprinkle with cornmeal.

On a lightly floured surface, roll each ball into a circle about 1/8 inch (3 mm) thick. For a successful grilled pizza the dough must be thin but not have any holes. (If you do tear a hole in the dough, simply press it back together.) Using both your hands, gently lift the dough onto the oiled baking sheet. Carry dough circles out to the grill and carefully lift the dough and stretch onto the hot grill. Grill for about 3 minutes, or until dough begins to bubble. Using tongs or a spatula, flip dough over and grill for another 2 minutes, just to set the dough on the bottom.

Turn off one side of the grill and move crust over the unlit burner. Brush top of crust with olive oil. Arrange toppings over the crust, ending with cheese. Close lid and let heat circulate to melt cheese and finish cooking bottom. If cheese melts before the bottom is lightly charred and crispy, move the pizza over the lit burner and grill briefly until done.

SERVES 4

✳ To roast garlic, wrap the unpeeled head in foil and roast on a medium grill, with the lid closed, for 25 to 30 minutes. Meanwhile, prepare the dough and toppings.

pumpkin amaretti ravioli

Pumpkin ravioli are a specialty of the northern region of Italy, and it was in a small restaurant in Parma that I had the best ravioli I've ever eaten in my life. This recipe pays homage to that very memorable lunch. I am taking some liberties by advising you to use ready-made dumpling wrappers (which I would spend time in jail for in Italy), but it saves a whole heap of time. The fragrant amaretti (almond) cookies give the pumpkin a hint of sweetness that blends brilliantly with the cream. Buon appetito!

1 tbsp. butter (15 mL)	**SAUCE**
1 oz. pancetta (30 g), finely diced	2 tbsp. butter (25 mL)
4 large shallots, finely chopped	6 shallots, chopped
1 clove garlic, chopped	leaves from 1/2 bunch fresh thyme sprigs, chopped
2 tsp. finely chopped fresh thyme (10 mL)	4 leaves fresh sage, finely chopped
1 tsp. finely chopped fresh sage (5 mL)	4 cups chicken stock (1 L)
freshly grated nutmeg to taste	2 cups whipping (35%) cream (500 mL)
salt and black pepper to taste	
1 can (28 oz./796 mL) pure pumpkin purée*	1/4 cup ground or crushed amaretti or other almond cookies (60 mL)
1 egg, lightly beaten	about 1/2 cup freshly grated Grana Padano or Parmigiano-Reggianno (125 mL)
40 (3-inch/8 cm) dumpling or perogy wrappers**	
1 egg, beaten	
ground semolina, for sprinkling	

In a large skillet over medium-high heat, melt the butter. Sauté pancetta until lightly browned. Add shallots; sauté for 3 to 4 minutes, or until soft and golden. Add the garlic, thyme, sage and nutmeg. Sauté until garlic is golden. Remove from heat and season with salt and pepper. Stir in the pumpkin purée. Let cool. Stir in 1 beaten egg, reserving a small amount.

Brush the edge of a dumpling wrapper lightly with some remaining beaten egg. Place 1 tsp. (5 mL) of filling on one half of wrapper, close to the middle. Fold dough over, creating a semi-circle. Press out air and pinch edges securely with a fork. Place on a baking sheet, not touching each other, and sprinkle with some semolina so they don't stick together.

Bring a large pot of salted water to a gentle boil for cooking ravioli.

Meanwhile, make the sauce. In a large skillet over medium-high heat, melt the butter. Sauté shallots, thyme and sage until shallots are just soft, 2 to 3 minutes. Stir in stock and cream; boil, without stirring, until reduced by half, thick and creamy. Keep sauce warm.

Cook ravioli for 3 to 4 minutes, or until tender. Drain immediately and toss in sauce. Serve ravioli immediately, sprinkled with amaretti and cheese.

SERVES 8

* Use only pure pumpkin purée, not pumpkin pie filling. If you can find smaller cans, the recipe is easy to divide in half for four people.

** You can also use wonton wrappers.

gnocchi with pecorino garlic butter

Great gnocchi are hard to come by, but perfect pillow-like gnocchi are hard not to share with everyone. These babies are light and fluffy but firm enough to keep their shape. The sauce is a simple combination of garlic, butter and pecorino cheese. The only daring part is mastering the dough itself. I make sure that I dry out the potatoes very well after mashing them and let them cool down. Some potatoes have more water than others, so if, after adding the flour and kneading, the dough still sticks to your hands, just sprinkle on a little more flour. I get right into making gnocchi and make a full batch (or more). I spread them on a baking sheet and freeze them overnight just like that. The next day I transfer them to zip-top plastic bags for easy retrieval on a rush night.

2 lb. Yukon Gold potatoes (1 kg)

1 1/3 cups all-purpose flour (325 mL)

2 eggs, lightly beaten

salt and pepper to taste

3 tbsp. butter (45 mL)

2 cloves garlic, chopped

1/3 cup chopped fresh parsley (75 mL)

1/4 cup grated pecorino (60 mL)

cracked black pepper to taste

In a large pot of lightly salted water, bring potatoes to a boil; cook until just tender when tested with a fork, 17 to 20 minutes. Drain potatoes and cool slightly. While still warm, peel potatoes and mash in a medium bowl. Spread mashed potatoes on a baking sheet to cool and allow steam to evaporate.

Meanwhile, bring a large pot of salted water to a boil for cooking gnocchi.

When potatoes are just warm, return them to the bowl. Make a well in centre of potatoes and sprinkle with the flour. Add the eggs. Using a fork, stir together flour and eggs, then gradually incorporate potato mixture until well blended. Season with salt and pepper.

Turn onto lightly floured surface and knead gently but thoroughly to develop a dough that is supple but not sticky, about 5 to 7 minutes, adding flour as needed. Divide dough into quarters. With your hands, gently roll each quarter into long strands about 1 inch (2.5 cm) thick. Using a sharp knife or pastry cutter, cut the strands into little rectangles (1 inch/2.5 cm long) that look like pillows. Lay gnocchi on a well-floured baking sheet and freeze immediately or cook right away.

Boil gnocchi for 2 to 3 minutes, or until they rise to the surface and still hold their shape. With a slotted spoon, transfer gnocchi to a bowl.

In a large skillet, melt the butter over high heat. Add garlic and sauté for 1 minute, or until garlic is just golden. Remove from heat and stir in parsley.

Add gnocchi to garlic butter and sprinkle with cheese and pepper. Toss gently to coat. Serve immediately.

SERVES 4 TO 6

squash and pinto bean roti

I put this in the daring category because some people are not that familiar with roti. In fact, they're quite easy to make. But you probably will have to go to a West Indian market to find the roti shells. You can use soft tortillas in a pinch, or even just make the filling and serve it with rice. These are hefty, so count on sharing.

3 tbsp. butter (45 mL)

1 large onion, chopped

1 small butternut squash,
    peeled and cut into 1-inch (2.5 cm) cubes

2 cloves garlic, chopped

1 cinnamon stick

1 tbsp. grated fresh ginger (15 mL)

2 tsp. cumin seeds (10 mL), ground

1 tsp. coriander seeds (5 mL), ground

1 tsp. chopped Thai chile or dried chile pepper (5 mL)

1/4 tsp. turmeric (1 mL)

pinch ground allspice

1/4 cup dry white wine (60 mL)

2 cups chicken stock (500 mL)

1/2 cup coconut milk (125 mL)

1 can (14 oz./398 mL) pinto beans, drained and rinsed

1/4 cup whole-milk yogurt (60 mL)

1/4 cup chopped fresh coriander (60 mL)

salt and black pepper to taste

2 large roti

In a medium saucepan, melt the butter over medium heat. Cook onion, stirring frequently, for 3 to 5 minutes, or until golden. Add squash, garlic, cinnamon stick, ginger, cumin seeds, coriander seeds, chile, turmeric and allspice. Cook, stirring occasionally, 5 minutes. Add wine and cook a further 5 minutes. Add stock and coconut milk; simmer, uncovered, for 15 to 20 minutes, or until squash is just tender and most of the liquid has evaporated.

Stir in the beans and cook 5 minutes just to develop flavour. Stir in the yogurt and fresh coriander; simmer for 5 more minutes. Season with salt and pepper. Discard cinnamon stick.

Spoon half of the filling into the middle of each roti. Fold in 2 sides each about 2 inches (5 cm). Roll the end closest to you over the filling, and continue to roll the roti, creating a package with the seam end down.

SERVES 2 OR 4

thai vegetable curry

This curry is loaded with unbelievably fragrant ingredients, but if you want to take the shortcut, buy a prepared Thai curry paste to replace the chiles, spices, lime leaves and ginger. Either way, the process is fairly simple. Making it from scratch just takes a little more time.

2 tbsp. vegetable oil (25 mL)	1 tsp. grated lime zest (5 mL)
5 shallots, chopped	1/2 tsp. anise seeds (2 mL), ground
2 large onions, chopped	1 1/2 cups coconut milk (375 mL)
3 cloves garlic, chopped	juice of 2 limes
3 red chiles, finely chopped	salt and black pepper to taste
1 tbsp. chopped fresh ginger (15 mL)	8 oz. firm tofu (250 g), cut into cubes
1 small banana, chopped	2 Asian eggplants, sliced crosswise
3 kaffir lime leaves, torn into strips	1/2 bunch broccoli, cut into florets
1 1/2 tsp. coriander seeds (7 mL), crushed	1/2 cup canned baby corn (125 mL)
1 tsp. cumin seeds (5 mL), crushed	1/2 cup frozen green peas (125 mL)
1 tsp. turmeric (5 mL)	fresh Thai basil leaves, for garnish

In a large saucepan over medium-high heat, heat the oil. Sauté the shallots and the onions for several minutes, or until soft. Add the garlic, chiles and ginger; sauté for several more minutes, until just soft. Add the banana, lime leaves, coriander seeds, cumin seeds, turmeric, lime zest, anise seeds, coconut milk and lime juice; stir well. Season with salt and pepper.

Reduce heat, cover and simmer, stirring occasionally, for 35 to 45 minutes, or until sauce is thick and reduced by half.

Meanwhile, fry tofu cubes; drain on paper towels. Fry eggplant slices; drain on paper towels. Blanch broccoli florets; drain.

Add the tofu, eggplant, broccoli, corn and peas to the curry. Bring to a gentle boil over medium heat and cook for 2 to 3 minutes, or until corn and peas are cooked. Season with salt and pepper. Add fresh whole basil leaves and serve with jasmine rice.

SERVES 4 TO 6

vegetable tempura

The possibilities for vegetables battered in tempura are immense. Go crazy! The whole trick is in the batter — use sparkling water for an extra-light texture and don't overmix it. Panko, Japanese bread crumbs available at sushi or specialty Asian stores, give the tempura that modern sculptured look.

1 small sweet potato, peeled, cut in half, thinly sliced

1 small head broccoli cut into florets

1 zucchini, thinly sliced

6 shiitake mushrooms, stems discarded

3 cups safflower or peanut oil (750 mL)

1/2 cup panko (Japanese bread crumbs) (125 mL)

DIPPING SAUCE

1/4 cup good-quality soy sauce (80 mL)

1/4 cup mirin (60 mL) or rice vinegar + 1 tbsp. (15 mL) sugar

TEMPURA BATTER

1/2 cup rice flour (125 mL)

1/4 cup cornstarch (60 mL)

1 tsp. baking powder (5 mL)

pinch each salt and sugar

1/2 cup + 2 tbsp. cold sparkling water (150 mL)

Boil sweet potato until tender; drain and let cool. Blanch broccoli florets for 2 minutes; drain and let cool. Dry sweet potato, broccoli and zucchini slices well on paper towels (the batter won't adhere to damp vegetables).

To make the dipping sauce, combine the soy sauce and mirin in a small bowl. Set aside.

To make the batter, blend the rice flour, cornstarch, baking powder, salt and sugar in a medium bowl. Add the sparkling water and stir with chopsticks or a fork. Do not overmix or the batter will be heavy and dense; there should be some small lumps in the batter, but break up any large lumps.

In a deep-fryer or large, heavy pot, heat oil to 375°F. Line a tray with paper towels. Put the panko in a shallow dish.

Working with about 5 pieces of vegetable at a time, gently dip each piece into batter and dredge in panko. Deep-fry until golden, 2 to 3 minutes. Using a slotted spoon, transfer tempura to the tray to drain. Make sure oil returns to 375°F between batches. Dredge and cook remaining tempura. Serve immediately with dipping sauce.

SERVES 4 TO 6

my mom's cod fish cakes

What can I say? This is my mom's secret recipe for crispy cod cakes. I call it secret because she didn't actually have a recipe; I had to develop one based on what she told me. The batter should be the right balance of potato (for a light texture) and some flour (to bind it). I have also made these fish cakes with fresh cod that I just chop up. It saves some time, since the salt cod needs to be soaked in water for two days. These cod cakes are a huge family tradition. You have to eat them fast or you won't get any!

7 oz. salt cod (200 g)

1 large Yukon Gold potato

3 eggs

3 green onions, finely chopped

3 tbsp. all-purpose flour (45 mL)

freshly cracked black pepper

1 tbsp. chopped fresh flat-leaf parsley (15 mL)

1/2 cup vegetable oil (125 mL)

Soak salt cod in water for at least 24 hours, changing the water several times.

Boil the potato until tender; mash it and let cool.

Coarsely chop the fish and place in a bowl. Stir in the mashed potato, eggs, green onions, pepper, flour and parsley.

Heat vegetable oil in a medium skillet over medium-high heat until hot but not smoking. Working in batches so you don't crowd the pan, scoop up a heaping tablespoonful of the fish mixture and put it in the oil. Cook for 3 to 4 minutes, or until fish cakes are golden on the bottom. Turn cakes and cook the other side until golden, another 3 to 4 minutes. Drain fish cakes on paper towels.

MAKES 16 TO 18 CAKES, SERVING 6 TO 8

fishing-trip smoked trout

Okay, the fishing trip could be just to your local fish market, but even so this is a cool little recipe for enjoying your own in-house smoked trout. The outdoor grill will work best, but you can also do it in your kitchen if you have an indoor smoking contraption. The marinade starts to cure the fish, and then the fish completely cooks while it's smoking over the hickory chips.

1 clove garlic, chopped

1 small shallot, sliced

zest and juice of 1/2 orange

leaves from several sprigs fresh thyme, chopped

3 tbsp. olive oil (45 mL)

1 tbsp. vodka (15 mL)

1 tsp. kosher salt (5 mL)

freshly cracked black pepper to taste

2 rainbow trout fillets, skin on

hickory smoking chips

In a shallow pan, whisk together the garlic, shallot, orange zest, orange juice, thyme, oil, vodka, salt and pepper. Add trout fillets, turning to coat. Make sure fish is immersed. Marinate at room temperature for 30 minutes.

Preheat grill to high.

Place hickory chips in a shallow container and place it on the main rack of the grill. Close lid and let hickory chips smoke for about 4 minutes.

Oil the grill and place it on the upper rack (where you'd normally keep things warm). Place fish on upper rack with skin down. Reduce heat to medium and close lid. Grill trout for 12 to 15 minutes, or until firm to the touch.

Serve at room temperature.

SERVES 4

dark ale–battered halibut and chips

I can't tell you for how many years I've wanted to make the perfect fish and chips. I think I've finally succeeded, and I'm asking you to treat this recipe as though it were a science project. You can change the fish — try cod, grouper or bass — but I wouldn't mess with the batter, the temperature or the thickness of the fish. (I tried it with a thicker piece and it just doesn't cook through the middle.) One more requirement: wash down the fish and chips with a pint. Eh, mate!

TARTAR SAUCE

1 cup mayonnaise (250 mL)

2 tbsp. chopped fresh parsley (25 mL)

1 tbsp. drained capers (15 mL), chopped

1 tsp. Dijon mustard (5 mL)

6 French gherkins or pickles, finely chopped

grated zest and juice of 1 lemon

salt and black pepper to taste

CHIPS

4 cups vegetable oil (1 L)

2 lb. Yukon Gold potatoes, peeled,
cut into 3-inch (8 cm) by 1/3-inch (8 mm) sticks,
soaked in cold water overnight and patted dry

salt to taste

FISH

1 3/4 cups sifted all-purpose flour (425 mL)

2 tsp. baking powder (10 mL)

1 tsp. salt (5 mL)

large pinch cayenne

2 egg whites

1 bottle dark ale

8 skinless halibut fillets
(each 3 oz./75 g and 1/2 inch/1 cm thick

salt and black pepper to taste

lemon wedges, for garnish

To make the tartar sauce, combine all the sauce ingredients in a bowl. Cover and refrigerate until needed. (Tartar sauce can be made several days ahead.)

To make the chips, in a large, heavy-bottomed pot, heat vegetable oil to 320°F. Working in small batches, cook the chips until soft and cooked through but not browned, about 3 minutes. Make sure oil returns to 320°F between batches. Drain on paper towels and let cool to room temperature.

Preheat oven to 150°F.

To make the batter, whisk together the flour, baking powder, salt, cayenne, egg whites and beer until smooth.

Heat oil to 375°F and fry chips in small batches until crisp and golden, 1 to 2 minutes. Drain on a rack over a baking sheet and immediately season with salt. Keep chips warm in the oven. Make sure oil returns to 375°F between batches.

Reduce oil to 365°F. Season the halibut with salt and pepper. Working with a few pieces at a time, dip the halibut in the batter and fry until golden and cooked through, turning once halfway through the cooking time, about 7 minutes total. Drain on paper towels and season immediately with salt. Make sure oil returns to 365°F between batches.

Serve fish with the chips, tartar sauce and lemon wedges.

SERVES 4

arctic char stuffed with orange, herbs and red onions

Arctic char is such a versatile fish, and because it's a little smaller than salmon, it's easier to deal with whole on the grill. Its flavour is a delicious cross between a delicate rainbow trout and a heavier salmon. I love it. This recipe will show off your grilling prowess. Feel free to experiment with the filling. Once grilled, the fish is crispy and brown on the outside and looks incredible presented on a big wooden plank.

1 tbsp. + 2 tsp. grape seed oil (15 mL + 10 mL)

1 red onion, sliced

1-inch piece fresh ginger (2.5 cm), julienned

1/2 small jalapeño, thinly sliced

1 orange, unpeeled and thinly sliced

juice of 1/2 lemon

2 tsp. Dijon mustard (10 mL)

2 Arctic char fillets, skin on (each 1 lb./500 g)

salt and cracked black pepper to taste

several sprigs fresh coriander

several fresh chives

Preheat grill to medium-high.

In a large skillet, heat 1 tbsp. (15 mL) of the oil over medium-high heat. Sauté the onion for 4 to 5 minutes, or until soft and golden. Add the ginger and jalapeño; sauté for 3 minutes. Remove from heat and set aside.

Grill orange slices for 2 minutes per side, or until grill marks are light brown. Set aside.

In a small bowl, stir together lemon juice and mustard.

Season fillets on both sides with salt and pepper. Lay 1 fillet, skin side down, on a baking sheet. Brush with half the lemon juice mixture. Arrange half the orange slices and half the coriander and chives evenly on the fish. Top with onion mixture, spreading evenly. Arrange remaining orange slices and herbs over top. Brush flesh side of remaining fillet with remaining lemon juice mixture. Lay on top of stuffing, skin side up.

Tightly tie fillets together with butcher's twine, using a criss–cross pattern to secure. Brush with remaining 2 tsp. (10 mL) oil.

Grill fish, turning just once (I use two large offset spatulas), for 6 to 7 minutes per side, or until a knife inserted into middle of stuffing is just warm. Reduce heat if skin is browning too rapidly.

Without removing string, slice fish into 6 to 8 thick pieces. Serve immediately.

SERVES 6 TO 8

brined roasted turkey with herbs and garlic

Everyone is talking about brining these days. I was skeptical before I developed this recipe, but I tell you, it rules! Brining makes the meat so tender and soft and gives it a more intense flavour. My family was literally hanging over the roasting pan picking at the last bits of meat. To properly test the doneness of the turkey, use a meat thermometer and don't go by the regular weight and time charts. The turkey can be brined the day before, rinsed and dried after the 6 hours and refrigerated until you roast it the next day.

12 cups water (3 L)
4 cups sugar (1 L)
1 1/2 cups kosher salt (375 mL)
1 young turkey (about 12 lb./5.5 kg)
2 tbsp. butter (25 mL), softened
several sprigs each fresh thyme, rosemary and sage
5 cloves garlic, slivered
freshly cracked black pepper
juice of 1/2 lemon

In a pot large enough to hold the turkey immersed in liquid, combine water, sugar and salt. Discard giblets and rinse turkey inside and out. Place in brine, breast side down. Make sure turkey is covered with brining liquid. Cover and refrigerate for 6 hours.

Preheat oven to 350°F.

Remove turkey and discard brine. Rinse turkey and pat dry. Carefully run your fingers under the breast skin to separate the skin from the flesh, being careful not to tear the skin. Rub breast meat with half the butter and push half of the herb sprigs evenly under skin. Press down on the skin to level it and to smooth out butter.

Put garlic and remaining herbs in the cavity. Season turkey with pepper and rub with remaining butter. Rub with lemon juice. Truss legs tightly with butcher's twine. Transfer to large roasting pan.

Roast, without basting, for 2 1/2 to 3 hours, or until a meat thermometer inserted in thickest part of thigh reads 180°F. Let turkey rest for 15 minutes before carving.

SERVES 8

braised duck with cipollini onions, cinnamon and amarone

Pack your bags, because I'm taking you to Venice. It's a well-kept secret that duck is very popular there. I go crazy over this recipe. Here I've combined lots of robust fresh herbs with Amarone — a red wine made with dried grapes — and cinnamon. The preparation is not particularly fussy. It just takes time to assemble all your ingredients and to slowly braise the duck. If you want to get more daring, grill the duck breasts instead. That way you can have rare breast alongside braised leg meat.

1 duck (about 4 lb./2 kg)	1 cinnamon stick
salt and black pepper to taste	2 bay leaves
3 tbsp. butter (45 mL)	3 whole cloves
1 lb. cipollini onions, blanched and peeled	6 sprigs fresh thyme
1 oz. pancetta or bacon (30 g),	2 sprigs fresh rosemary
cut into 1/2-inch (1 cm) pieces	1/3 cup golden raisins (75 mL)
1 leek, washed and sliced	2 cups Amarone or other dry red wine (500 mL)
2 stalks celery, diced	1 can (28 oz./796 mL) crushed plum tomatoes with juice
2 carrots, diced	2 cups chicken stock or water (500 mL)

Trim duck of excess fat and cut into 8 serving pieces; save the bones for stock, if desired. Season with salt and pepper.

Melt half of the butter in a large, heavy-bottomed casserole over medium-high heat. Brown duck evenly, about 3 minutes per side. Drain off excess fat, if desired. Transfer duck to a plate.

Melt remaining butter in the casserole. Cook onions, stirring frequently, until golden, about 3 minutes. Add the pancetta; cook, stirring frequently, until pancetta is golden. Add leek, celery and carrots; cook for a couple of minutes. Return duck to casserole and add the cinnamon stick, bay leaves, cloves, thyme, rosemary, raisins and wine. Bring to a boil, reduce heat and simmer gently, uncovered, for about 30 minutes, or until wine is reduced by half.

Add the tomatoes and stock. Season with salt and pepper. Bring to a boil, then reduce heat to low. Cover and simmer for about 1 hour, turning the duck often, until duck is very tender.

If desired, remove cinnamon, bay leaves and herb sprigs from the sauce. (I don't bother, personally.) Serve duck with the sauce.

SERVES 4 TO 6

roasted pork loin with sour cherry marinade

I first made this pork roast on the beach in Malibu. (I know, I know, the sympathy cards are rolling in.) I was on a photo shoot for a food magazine and we were shooting the summer issue. The pork works best on a rotisserie, because the juices naturally baste the meat. If you're cooking over charcoal, it's even more flavourful. That doesn't mean you can't make it in the oven, though. Also, the basting sauce has plenty of room for interpretation. You can use blueberries, sour apples or even blackberries.

BASTING SAUCE
1 bouquet garni (handful of juniper berries,
   handful of allspice berries and 2 bay leaves)
2 1/2 cups apple cider (625 mL)
1 1/2 cups Riesling or other dry white wine (375 mL)
1/2 cup dried sour cherries (125 mL)
1/4 cup apple butter or sweet apple sauce (60 mL)
2 cloves garlic, minced

1 large onion, finely chopped
whole leaves from 8 sprigs fresh thyme
freshly cracked black pepper to taste

1 bone-in pork loin (about 5 lb./2.2 kg)
salt and freshly cracked black pepper to taste
2 Golden Delicious apples
2 tbsp. butter (25 mL)

To make bouquet garni, place spices in a small piece of cheesecloth and tie together with butcher's twine.

In a large saucepan, combine remaining basting sauce ingredients. Add the bouquet garni. Bring to a boil, reduce heat to medium and simmer, uncovered, 20 minutes. Strain the sauce, separately reserving the solids and the liquid. Discard bouquet garni.

Preheat grill to medium-high. Season pork loin with salt and pepper and place loin on rotisserie rod. Grill-roast the pork, basting frequently with the reserved basting liquid, for 2 hours, or until a meat thermometer inserted into the centre of the roast reads 160°F. (Alternately, roast in a 350°F oven until a meat thermometer reads 160°F.) Transfer roast to a cutting board, cover loosely with foil and let rest for 15 minutes before carving.

Meanwhile, peel and chop apples. In a medium saucepan, melt butter over high heat. Sauté apples for 4 minutes, or until just tender. Add reserved solids and remaining basting liquid. Reduce heat to low and simmer for 5 minutes. Remove from heat and adjust seasoning.

Slice pork and serve with sauce.

SERVES 8

venison with rioja sauce

If you're looking for something that your friends have probably never tasted, this is the dish. Venison has a lean, gamy flavour that takes an earthy turn with this Spanish red wine and mushroom sauce. If you really want to be daring, try grating a very small amount of bittersweet chocolate over the venison just before serving. It's absolutely wild. If you can't find a Rioja, try a Zinfandel or maybe a fruity red in its place.

1 oz. dried porcini mushrooms (30 g)

3 tbsp. vegetable oil (40 mL)

1 leek, white part only

1 rack venison (1 1/2 lb./750 g)

salt and freshly cracked black pepper to taste

2 tbsp. butter (30 mL)

3 medium Portobello mushrooms, stems discarded, diced

1/3 cup cipollini onions (75 mL), peeled and cut in half

1 large clove garlic, cut in half

2/3 cup Rioja or other dry red wine (150 mL)

2 cups veal stock (500 mL)

2 tsp. Worcestershire sauce (10 mL)

leaves from 5 sprigs fresh thyme, chopped

1/2 tsp. chopped fresh sage (2 mL)

1 1/2 tbsp. cassis or sweet sherry (20 mL)

Preheat oven to 400°F.

Soak dried porcini mushrooms in 1 cup (250 mL) of hot water for 30 minutes. Drain mushrooms, reserving 1/2 cup (125 mL) of the soaking liquid.

Meanwhile, oil a small roasting pan or baking sheet with 1 1/2 tbsp. (20 mL) of the vegetable oil. Cut leek in half lengthwise and wash well. Place in roasting pan and roast for 15 minutes or until leeks are golden and soft. Dice leeks and set aside.

Heat a large ovenproof skillet over high heat. Add remaining 1 1/2 tbsp. (20 mL) vegetable oil. Season venison with salt and pepper. Sear venison on all sides. Transfer skillet to middle rack of oven and roast venison for 18 minutes for rare, or until a meat thermometer reads 125°F. Let venison rest for 15 minutes before carving.

While venison is roasting, make the sauce. Heat a large, heavy-bottomed saucepan over medium heat. Melt 1 1/2 tbsp. (20 mL) of the butter. Brown the Portobello and porcini mushrooms. Remove mushrooms and set aside. Reduce heat to low. In the same saucepan, melt the remaining 1/2 tbsp. (10 mL) butter. Add the cipollini onions; cook, stirring, for 10 to 12 minutes, or until brown. Add garlic and cook, stirring, for 2 minutes.

Increase heat to high. Deglaze pan with wine. Reduce wine to 1/4 cup (60 mL).

Stir in veal stock and reserved mushroom soaking liquid. Bring to a boil. Reduce heat to medium and cook for 3 minutes. Add sautéed mushrooms, roasted leeks and Worcestershire sauce. Boil gently, stirring occasionally, until sauce is reduced by half, 15 to 20 minutes. Stir in any venison pan drippings, the thyme, sage, cassis and black pepper. Cook for a further 10 minutes. Adjust seasoning with salt.

Slice venison across the grain and serve with the Rioja sauce.

SERVES 4

garlic-studded prime rib roast

Prime rib is the king of roast beef. It's basically like eating many fat, juicy rib-eye steaks with the bone in. Prime rib is quite costly, but for a special occasion I can't think of a better cut. To make a perfect thing even better, I top it with an intense crust of mustard, cloves and juniper berries and stuff it jam packed with garlic slivers. Prime taste!

2 tbsp. juniper berries (25 mL)
1 tbsp. mustard seeds (15 mL)
7 whole cloves
3 tbsp. Dijon mustard (45 mL)
2 tbsp. chopped fresh thyme (25 mL)
salt and freshly ground pepper to taste
1 bone-in prime rib roast (6 lb./2.5 kg)
4 medium cloves garlic, cut in quarters lengthwise

Preheat oven to 400°F.

Finely grind the juniper berries, mustard seeds and cloves in a spice grinder or with a mortar and pestle. Mix with Dijon mustard, thyme, salt and pepper.

Make small incisions (big enough to fit a quartered piece of garlic clove) all over the prime rib. Insert garlic pieces into the holes. Place roast in a roasting pan and rub all over with the spice paste.

Roast for 25 minutes. Reduce heat to 350°F and roast for 1 1/2 hours, or until internal temperature reaches 135°F for a rare roast. Transfer roast to a cutting board and let rest for 15 minutes before carving.

SERVES 10 TO 12

sweet
science

Now that you've mustered up the ner

to gauge your own pinch size,

pull back the reins and step into baking mod

Taking chances simply does not apply to baking

When the recipe says 3/4 tsp. baking soda,

make sure you have precisely that amount.

Baking is a science, and to win sweetpoin

we have to follow the rules.

These recipes are arranged from

easiest to most challenging and include

some of my absolute favourites.

Add your own twists with garnishes or sauces — jus

don't alter the main component of the dessert

vanilla rum tipsy bananas

I figure these bananas have to be tipsy after being doused with all that dark rum. This is such a creamy combination when the sugars start to caramelize with the bananas, and the lime juice gives it a tangy hit. Two more words that describe this dish: eee zee.

1/3 cup dark rum (75 mL)
2 tbsp. brown sugar (25 mL)
juice of 1 lime
1 vanilla bean
4 medium bananas
whipped cream, for garnish
grilled lime slices, for garnish

Preheat grill to medium. Cut 4 large rectangles of foil.

In a small bowl, combine the rum, brown sugar and lime juice. Cut the vanilla bean in half lengthwise and scrape the seeds into the rum mixture. Stir well.

Cut bananas in half lengthwise but not all the way through, so they are "hinged."

Place each banana on a piece of foil. Score each banana crosswise about 4 times along its length. Pour rum mixture equally into the slits. Wrap each banana tightly in foil.

Grill bananas for 8 to 10 minutes, or until just starting to soften.

Transfer bananas to serving plates. Drizzle with any juices collected in the foil. Garnish with a dollop of cream and grilled lime slices.

SERVES 4

blackberry peach crisp

Summer is the best time to make this fruity crisp that contrasts sweet, juicy peaches with tart, crunchy blackberries. It's also a great dessert for beginners who don't feel like being too technical. You can freely substitute just about any berry for the blackberries.

FILLING

6 large freestone peaches

1 pint blackberries (500 mL)

1/3 cup sugar (75 mL)

2 tbsp. cornstarch (25 mL)

grated zest of 1 lemon

TOPPING

1/2 cup quick-cooking rolled oats (125 mL)

1/4 cup all-purpose flour (60 mL)

1/3 cup cold butter (75 mL), cut into chunks

1/3 cup brown sugar (75 mL)

1/4 cup raw pistachios (60 mL), chopped

1/2 tsp. cinnamon (2 mL)

pinch ground cloves

Preheat oven to 350°F. Generously butter a 9 1/2- by 8-inch baking dish.

Peel the peaches: immerse in boiling water for 10 seconds and then plunge immediately into cold water. Peel. Cut peaches into 1-inch (2.5 cm) chunks and transfer to a large bowl. Add remaining filling ingredients. Toss to blend.

To make the topping, in a food processor combine the oats, flour and cold butter. Pulse several times until mixture resembles coarse meal. Transfer to a bowl and add remaining topping ingredients. Stir well.

Transfer fruit to the baking dish. Spoon the topping over filling, covering it completely. Bake for 40 to 45 minutes, or until bubbly and golden.

SERVES 6 TO 8

banana chocolate bread pudding

Just when I thought you couldn't improve on perfection, I added caramelized bananas and chocolate to a creamy bread pudding. This is a great dessert if you're a beginner or you don't feel like fussing.

10 slices egg bread, 1/2 inch (1 cm) thick,
    a few days old
2 tbsp. melted butter (25 mL)
6 eggs
2 cups whole milk (500 mL)
2 cups table (18%) cream (500 mL)
1/2 cup + 1/3 cup sugar (125 mL + 75 mL)
1 tsp. vanilla (5 mL) or seeds from 1/2 vanilla bean
1/2 tsp. cinnamon (2 mL)
freshly grated nutmeg to taste

pinch salt
1/4 cup butter (60 mL)
4 ripe bananas, sliced
2 tbsp. dark rum (25 mL)

CHOCOLATE SAUCE
4 oz. bittersweet chocolate (120 g), finely chopped
3/4 cup milk (175 mL)
3 tbsp. dark rum (45 mL)

Butter a 9- by 13-inch baking dish.

Brush 5 slices of the bread with melted butter; set aside. Break remaining bread into bite-sized pieces.

In a medium bowl, combine the eggs, milk, cream, 1/2 cup (125 mL) of the sugar, vanilla, cinnamon, nutmeg and salt. Whisk to blend. Set aside.

In a large skillet, melt butter over high heat. Stir in remaining 1/3 cup (75 mL) sugar. Cook, stirring, for 2 to 3 minutes, or until golden caramel forms. Add the banana slices and toss for 2 minutes, or until just soft and golden. Stir in rum. Remove from heat and let cool slightly.

Preheat oven to 325°F.

Arrange broken bread pieces in baking dish and spoon bananas on top, spreading evenly. Cover with buttered bread slices in a single layer. Pour egg mixture over top. Press bread down and let stand for 30 minutes.

Bake for 35 to 40 minutes, or until puffed and golden but custard is still moist in centre.

Meanwhile, make chocolate sauce. Combine sauce ingredients in a medium stainless steel bowl and place over (not in) a pot of gently simmering water until chocolate melts. Stir until smooth.

Serve pudding warm with warm sauce.

SERVES 12

individual carrot cakes with lemon mascarpone icing

This entire cake is made in the food processor and is foolproof. It's moist and fragrant and looks like you worked all day (but you didn't). The mascarpone cheese makes the icing especially creamy, but you can use regular cream cheese (if you must). This cake is amazing!

4 eggs	**ICING**
1 1/2 cups sugar (375 mL)	1/2 cup mascarpone cheese (125 mL)
1 cup vegetable oil (250 mL)	finely grated zest of 1 lemon
3 tbsp. apple butter (45 mL)	1/2 cup whipping (35%) cream (125 mL)
1 tsp. vanilla (5 mL)	1/4 cup icing sugar (60 mL)
2 cups all-purpose flour (500 mL)	2 tbsp. lemon juice (25 mL)
1 1/2 tsp. baking powder (7 mL)	1/2 tsp. vanilla (2 mL)
1 1/2 tsp. pumpkin pie spice (7 mL)	
1 tsp. cinnamon (5 mL)	
1/2 tsp. baking soda (2 mL)	
pinch allspice	
1 lb. carrots, peeled and grated (500 g)	
1/2 cup chopped walnuts (125 mL)	
1/2 cup unsweetened grated coconut (125 mL)	

Preheat oven to 350°F. Spray 12 individual Bundt cake pans or two 10-inch (25 cm) cake pans with nonstick cooking spray.

In a food processor, combine eggs, sugar, oil, apple butter and vanilla; blend well. In a bowl, sift together flour, baking powder, pumpkin pie spice, cinnamon, baking soda and allspice. Add dry ingredients to food processor and pulse several times until smooth. Scrape down sides of bowl and pulse to blend.

Combine carrots, walnuts and coconut in medium bowl; stir well. Pour batter into carrot mixture and stir to combine well. Pour mixture into cake pans and bake for 25 to 35 minutes, or until tester comes out clean. (If making 10-inch cakes, bake for 35 to 40 minutes, or until tester comes out clean.) Cool on wire rack.

To make the icing, in a stand mixer fitted with the paddle attachment, beat mascarpone until smooth. Add remaining ingredients and beat on medium speed until well combined. Spread icing over cooled cake.

MAKES 12 INDIVIDUAL BUNDT CAKES OR TWO 10-INCH CAKES

walnut buttermilk cake with honey lemon glaze

This recipe is a variation on a traditional Greek cake that I love. It's perfect as a coffee cake. My version is more tangy with the addition of lemon zest and not as sweet, with less sugar and honey. The buttermilk gives it a supple texture.

1/2 cup butter (125 mL), at room temperature
1 1/4 cups sugar (300 mL)
4 eggs, separated
grated zest of 2 lemons
1 tsp. vanilla (5 mL)
1 cup all-purpose flour (250 mL)
2 tsp. baking powder (10 mL)
1/2 tsp. baking soda (2 mL)
1/4 tsp. salt (1 mL)
3 1/2 oz. ground walnuts (100 g)
3/4 cup buttermilk (175 mL)

GLAZE
1/2 cup water (125 mL)
1/4 cup honey (60 mL)
1/4 cup sugar (60 mL)
juice of 1 lemon

Preheat oven to 350°F. Trace the bottom of a 10-inch (25 cm) cake pan onto parchment paper and cut out the circle. Fit parchment paper into pan. (The sides of the pan don't need to be buttered.)

In a large bowl and using an electric mixer on medium speed, cream butter with half of the sugar until light and fluffy, about 5 minutes. Add egg yolks 1 at a time, beating well after each addition until well blended. Beat in lemon zest and vanilla.

In a medium bowl, sift flour, baking powder, baking soda and salt. Stir in ground walnuts. With mixer on medium speed, add dry ingredients to batter alternately with buttermilk in three batches, beginning and ending with dry. Scrape down sides and beat on high speed for another minute to develop cake's structure.

In a separate clean, stainless steel bowl, whip egg whites until soft peaks begin to form. Gradually beat in the remaining sugar in a steady stream until stiff peaks hold. Gently but thoroughly fold egg whites into batter until no whites can be seen.

Pour batter into pan and bake for 35 to 40 minutes, or until tester inserted in middle comes out dry. Let cool completely on rack and then remove from pan.

To make the glaze, in a small saucepan, combine glaze ingredients. Cook, stirring, over medium heat just until sugar dissolves and mixture just comes to a boil. Let cool slightly, then brush cooled cake with warm glaze.

SERVES 10 TO 12

strawberry rhubarb shortcakes

These little cakes are a mouthful of spring. When rhubarb season is just ending and strawberries make their appearance, this compote is a perfect balance of sweet and tangy. If you feel like a twist, serve these with a big scoop of vanilla ice cream instead of whipped cream.

STRAWBERRY RHUBARB SAUCE

1 pint fresh strawberries (500 mL), quartered

1 cup chopped fresh or frozen rhubarb (250 mL)

1/2 cup sugar (125 mL)

1 tbsp. cornstarch (15 mL)

SHORTCAKES

2 cups all-purpose flour (500 mL), sifted

1/4 cup sugar (60 mL)

1 1/2 tsp. baking powder (7 mL)

pinch salt

grated zest of 1 orange

1/3 cup cold butter (75 mL), cut into pieces

1/2 cup milk (125 mL)

1/4 cup whipping (35%) cream (60 mL)

2 tbsp. fresh orange juice (25 mL)

whipped cream (optional)

To make the sauce, combine all sauce ingredients in a medium saucepan. Bring to a boil, stirring with a wooden spoon, then reduce heat and simmer for 8 to 10 minutes, or until thick and glossy. Let cool.

Preheat oven to 375°F. Line a baking sheet with parchment paper.

To make the shortcakes, combine flour, sugar, baking powder, salt and orange zest in a large bowl. Using a pastry cutter or two knives, cut in cold butter until mixture resembles coarse meal. Stir together milk, cream and orange juice. Gradually add liquid to dry ingredients, stirring with a fork just until dough comes together.

On a lightly floured surface, roll dough out to a circle 3/4 inch (2 cm) thick. Using a cookie cutter, cut out 2 1/2-inch (6 cm) rounds. You should have 8 to 10 shortcakes. Place shortcakes on baking sheet. Bake for 20 to 30 minutes or until puffed and golden. Transfer to wire rack to cool slightly before serving.

Arrange shortcakes on serving plates. Spoon sauce over shortcakes and top with whipped cream, if desired.

MAKES 8 TO 10 CAKES

ice wine truffles

This great recipe will turn almost anyone into a home chocolate maker. Making truffles is usually a challenging process, but I've simplified the recipe so you don't have to dip or mould anything. The combination of ice wine and chocolate is second to none, but you can substitute other liqueurs if you don't happen to have a bottle open.

6 oz. good-quality bittersweet chocolate (175 g)
1/2 cup whipping (35%) cream (125 mL)
2 tbsp. ice wine (25 mL)
finely chopped almonds with skin to taste
good-quality cocoa powder

Chop the chocolate very finely and transfer to a medium bowl. Boil cream and immediately pour over chopped chocolate. Stir until all chocolate has melted. Stir in ice wine until blended. Cover surface with plastic wrap and freeze until firm, about 2 hours.

Scoop into small balls with a melon baller and transfer to a baking sheet. Freeze for 10 minutes. Roll truffles in almonds, then dust with cocoa powder.

MAKES ABOUT 20 TRUFFLES

venetian fritters

Every Mediterranean country has a version of these little fritters, which vary slightly depending on who makes them. They are at their crispy best when freshly fried and lightly dusted with icing sugar and cinnamon.

1 1/4 cups all-purpose flour (300 mL)

1/3 cup granulated sugar (75 mL)

2 tbsp. olive oil (25 mL)

1 tbsp. apple cider vinegar (15 mL)

1 egg

1 egg yolk

pinch salt

1 1/2 cups vegetable oil (375 mL)

1/4 cup icing sugar (60 mL)

cinnamon to taste

In a medium bowl, stir together the flour, granulated sugar, oil, vinegar, egg, egg yolk and salt. Turn out onto a lightly floured surface and knead until smooth, 3 to 5 minutes. Add a little extra flour if dough sticks to surface. Cover well and let rest 30 minutes.

On a lightly floured surface or in a pasta machine, roll dough into a sheet about 1/8 inch (3 mm) thick. With a pastry wheel or knife, cut into strips about 1 1/2 inches by 4 inches (4 cm by 10 cm).

Heat oil in a large skillet to 350°F. Fry fritters, about 6 at a time, turning with a slotted spoon, until evenly golden, 2 to 3 minutes. Drain on paper towels.

Transfer to a serving tray and dust generously with icing sugar and then cinnamon.

SERVES 8

honey lemon walnut puffs

These little puffs are like homemade doughnuts, deliciously light and crispy when they're fresh out of the fryer. I like to serve them warm drizzled with the honey lemon sauce and topped with walnuts. Major addiction factor!

1 1/4 cups + 1/4 cup all-purpose flour
   (300 mL + 60 mL)
1/2 pkg. instant yeast (1 tsp./5 mL)
1 tbsp. sugar (15 mL)
1 tsp. baking powder (5 mL)
1/2 tsp. salt (3 mL)
1/4 tsp. baking soda (1 mL)
1/4 tsp. ground allspice (1 mL)
1 egg

1/2 cup buttermilk (125 mL)
1/2 tsp. vanilla (2 mL)
1 cup (approx.) vegetable or peanut oil (250 mL)
1/4 cup chopped walnuts (60 mL)

SYRUP
1/2 cup Greek honey (125 mL)
juice of 1/2 lemon
1 cinnamon stick

In a medium bowl, combine 1 1/4 cups (300 mL) of the flour, the yeast, sugar, baking powder, salt, baking soda and allspice; stir until blended.

In a small bowl, beat the egg. Stir in buttermilk and vanilla. Add wet ingredients to flour mixture and stir until all flour has been incorporated. Batter will be sticky.

Lightly dust a surface with some of the remaining flour. Turn out dough and knead until smooth and slightly sticky to the touch, adding additional flour a little at a time as needed.

Dust a medium bowl with some flour and drop in dough ball. Cover with plastic and let rest until doubled, about 2 hours.

Meanwhile, make the syrup. In a small saucepan, combine the honey, lemon juice and cinnamon stick. Bring to a boil, stirring. Remove from heat and let stand until cool to the touch.

Punch down dough and turn onto lightly floured surface. With your hands, pat into a rough oval about 1/4 inch (5 mm) thick. Cut into 1 1/2-inch (4 cm) squares. Don't worry about being too exact — the puffs will take on a free-form shape as they cook.

Heat 3/4 inch (2 cm) oil in a small, heavy skillet until hot but not smoking. Drop about 6 puffs into hot oil and fry about 1 minute on each side, or until evenly browned. Drain on paper towels.

Drizzle warm puffs with honey syrup and sprinkle with walnuts.

SERVES 8 TO 10

py lemon roasted chicken, p. 133; oven-roasted potato wedges with rosemary, p. 119

baked pear with roquefort and port, p. 82

lemon crème brûlée tarts with chocolate shortbread crust, p. 196

almost flourless chocolate hazelnut cake with caramel sauce

This cake is my brother's absolute favourite, only I have to leave out the nuts because he's allergic to them. There is just enough flour to turn it from an ethereal mousse into a moist cake. The caramel sauce has a bitter edge that balances the rich whipped cream. Plan on doubling the recipe, because this cake disappears fast.

6 oz. bittersweet chocolate (175 g), finely chopped

3/4 cup unsalted butter (175 mL)

1/4 cup cake-and-pastry flour (60 mL), sifted

1 tbsp. cocoa powder (15 mL)

1/4 cup coarsely chopped toasted hazelnuts (60 mL)

5 eggs, separated

1/2 tsp. vanilla (2 mL)

2/3 cup + 2 tbsp. sugar (150 mL + 25 mL)

pinch salt

1 1/2 cups whipping (35%) cream (375 mL), whipped

CARAMEL SAUCE

1/2 cup sugar (125 mL)

1/2 cup whipping (35%) cream (125 mL)

2 tbsp. brandy (25 mL)

Preheat oven to 350°F. Trace the bottom of a 9-inch (23 cm) springform pan onto parchment paper and cut out the circle. Fit parchment paper into pan. Melt chocolate and butter together in a double boiler. Stir until smooth. Let cool slightly.

Sift together flour and cocoa. Stir in hazelnuts. In a large bowl, whisk together egg yolks, vanilla and 2/3 cup (150 mL) of the sugar until smooth and pale. Slowly whisk melted chocolate into yolk mixture until smooth. Fold in flour mixture.

In a separate clean bowl, beat egg whites until soft peaks hold. Continue beating whites while slowly adding remaining 2 tbsp. (25 mL) sugar and salt. Fold whites gently but thoroughly into batter.

Pour batter into prepared pan. Bake on middle rack for 40 to 45 minutes, or until firm but still spongy in the middle. Let cool completely on wire rack. (Cake will fall.) Run a knife along the sides of the pan to release cake from edges and remove cake from pan.

To make the caramel sauce, heat sugar in a narrow, heavy-bottomed saucepan with high sides. Over medium-high heat, cook sugar until it melts, tipping and gently swirling the pot to prevent scorching. Cook until sugar begins to turn a caramel colour, 4 to 5 minutes. (Make sure caramel does not begin to smoke.) Immediately remove from heat and pour in cream. (Careful — the mixture will bubble up.) Do not stir. Let stand 2 or 3 minutes. When bubbles subside, add brandy and stir until combined. Let cool. To serve, slice cake and top with a dollop of whipped cream. Drizzle with caramel sauce.

SERVES 8

maple cheesecake with blackberry sauce

I felt like a change in my usual cheesecake so I just threw in some maple syrup and gave it a blackberry sauce. Since there is no flour (that is, structure) in the filling, it will collapse slightly. To avoid that completely, you can wrap the springform pan in foil and bake the whole thing in a water bath. This will regulate the temperature and keep the custard from rising. I find it a bit easier to just bake it at a lower temperature and let it cool inside the oven with the door open. Try both and see which you like best.

CRUST
1 cup graham cracker crumbs (250 mL)

1/4 cup melted butter (60 mL)

1/2 tsp. cinnamon (2 mL)

FILLING
1 lb. cream cheese (500 g), at room temperature

3/4 cup sugar (175 mL)

6 eggs, separated

1/4 cup sour cream (60 mL)

juice of 1/2 lemon

grated zest of 1 lemon

1/4 cup maple syrup (60 mL)

1 tsp. vanilla (5 mL)

3 tbsp. cornstarch (45 mL)

BLACKBERRY SAUCE
3 cups fresh or frozen blackberries (750 mL)

1/4 cup sugar (125 mL)

1 tbsp. lemon juice (15 mL)

1 tsp. cornstarch (5 mL)

Trace the bottom of a 9-inch (23 cm) springform pan onto parchment paper and cut out the circle. Butter the bottom and sides of pan. Fit parchment circle into pan. Butter the paper.

To make the crust, combine crumbs, butter and cinnamon in a bowl. Stir well. Press the crust evenly into bottom of pan, pressing to secure. Chill while you make the filling.

Preheat oven to 275°F. In a stand mixer fitted with the paddle attachment, beat cream cheese with sugar until smooth. Add the egg yolks 3 at a time and beat on low, beating well after each addition. Scrape down sides of bowl. Add the sour cream, lemon juice and zest, maple syrup and vanilla. Blend until smooth. Add the cornstarch and blend until smooth.

In a clean stainless steel bowl, whip the egg whites until soft peaks hold. Fold egg whites gently but thoroughly into cheese mixture, making sure no streaks of egg white remain.

Pour batter into pan. Bake in middle of oven for about 1 hour and 50 minutes, or until cheesecake is just firm. Increase temperature to 300°F. Cook another 15 minutes, or until cake is golden. Turn oven off and open door slightly. Leave cake in the oven for 30 minutes. Remove and let cool completely on a rack.

To make the sauce, combine all sauce ingredients in a small saucepan. Bring to a boil over medium heat, stirring constantly. Reduce heat to low and simmer, stirring, for 5 minutes, or until sauce is slightly thickened and glossy. Press sauce through a fine-mesh sieve set over a bowl and let cool.

Serve cheesecake with sauce.

SERVES 12 TO 14

sticky pumpkin date pudding with bourbon toffee sauce

Traditionally this is a steamed pudding, but I actually bake it instead. It's moist enough that it turns out like a soft cake. I made it for a Food Network function one fall and it seemed to be the hit of the dessert plate. You probably won't be able to eat just one, and you'll be licking the plate for the last of the sauce!

1/3 cup chopped and packed dates (75 mL)

1/4 cup chopped and packed black dried figs (60 g)

1 cup water (250 mL)

1 tsp. baking soda (5 mL)

1/2 cup pure pumpkin purée (125 mL)

3/4 cup all-purpose flour (175 mL), sifted

1 tsp. cinnamon (5 mL)

1/2 tsp. baking powder (2 mL)

1/4 tsp. ground allspice (1 mL)

pinch freshly grated nutmeg

pinch salt

1/3 cup butter (75 mL), softened

1/2 cup dark brown sugar (125 mL)

2 eggs, at room temperature

1/2 tsp. vanilla (2 mL)

grated zest of 1 orange

BOURBON TOFFEE SAUCE

1 tbsp. butter (15 mL)

1/4 cup brown sugar (60 mL)

1/3 cup whipping (35%) cream (75 mL)

2 tbsp. bourbon (25 mL)

Preheat oven to 350°F. Butter six 6-oz. (175 mL) ramekins.

In a medium saucepan, combine dates, figs and water. Cook, covered, for 15 to 20 minutes, or until fruit is soft and most of the water has evaporated. Purée in a blender. Return warm purée to the saucepan and stir in the baking soda. Stir in the pumpkin purée and set aside.

Sift together flour, cinnamon, baking powder, allspice, nutmeg and salt into a bowl or onto a sheet of wax paper.

In a large bowl with an electric mixer, cream butter with sugar until fluffy. Add the eggs, 1 at a time, beating well after each addition. Beat in vanilla and orange zest. Add the pumpkin mixture alternately with the flour mixture, beating on low speed until well blended.

Pour batter into ramekins or custard cups and bake for 20 to 25 minutes, or until a tester comes out clean.

Meanwhile, make the sauce. Melt butter in a medium saucepan over medium heat. Stir in the sugar and cook, stirring, for 3 to 4 minutes, or until bubbly and slightly thickened. Stir in cream and bourbon. Cook for 7 to 9 minutes, without stirring, until thick and syrupy.

Flip puddings out onto serving plates and drizzle with warm sauce.

SERVES 6

greek baked semolina custard with lemon honey syrup (galaktoboureko)

Of all Greek desserts, this has always been the one I get physical cravings for. I have reworked it many times over the years, but I think I've finally mastered it. I've reduced the copious quantities of sugar that most Greek versions use, and I've added real vanilla bean to the creamy custard. Once the crispy phyllo pie comes out of the oven and is drizzled with the tangy honey syrup, it honestly makes my mouth water. Good luck with having just one piece!

6 cups milk (1.5 L)

1 1/2 cups sugar (375 mL)

1 cup semolina (250 mL)

1 vanilla bean

5 eggs, lightly beaten

zest of 1 lemon

about 16 sheets phyllo

1/2 cup melted butter (125 mL)

cinnamon to taste

LEMON HONEY SYRUP

1 cup water (250 mL)

1/2 cup sugar (125 mL)

1/2 cup honey (preferably Greek thyme) (125 mL)

juice of 1/2 lemon

1 cinnamon stick

Preheat oven to 375°F.

In a large saucepan, combine milk, sugar and semolina. Scrape the seeds from the vanilla bean into the mixture. Stir constantly over medium heat until mixture comes to a boil and thickens, about 15 minutes. Remove from heat. Stir in eggs and lemon zest. Let cool for 10 minutes.

Arrange 1 phyllo sheet on a surface. (Keep remaining sheets covered under a damp tea towel.) Brush phyllo with melted butter. Top with another sheet and brush; repeat until you have a stack of 8 sheets. Arrange phyllo in bottom of rectangular baking pan. Pour in cooled custard.

Butter and stack another 8 phyllo sheets and arrange them over the custard. Make several cuts with a knife to allow steam to escape.

Bake in middle of oven for about 35 minutes, or until golden and custard has puffed. Let cool.

To make the syrup, in a small saucepan, bring all syrup ingredients to a boil. Reduce heat and simmer gently until slightly thickened and reduced by about one quarter. Cool slightly. Discard cinnamon stick.

Pour warm syrup to your liking over cooled custard. Sprinkle with cinnamon.

SERVES 8 TO 10

ruby grapefruit sabayon on coconut crust

Grapefruit are so versatile and yet so underrated. All the other citrus fruits get so much air time in desserts, but where is the grapefruit? This brilliant little ruby red citrus fruit is a burst of flavour on top of my chewy coconut crust. Cassis is a black currant liqueur. If you can't find it, use sweet sherry or another fruit liqueur. This dessert is definitely a show stopper for when you want to impress guests. To make it easier, bake the crusts the day before and store them in a dry place. All you have to do is make the sabayon just before serving, and you're laughing.

CRUST

3/4 cup shredded unsweetened coconut (175 mL)

1/4 cup graham cracker crumbs (60 mL)

1/4 cup sugar (60 mL)

3 tbsp. melted butter (45 mL)

1 tbsp. honey (15 mL)

1 tsp. grated grapefruit zest (5 mL)

SABAYON

6 egg yolks

1/3 cup sugar (75 mL)

1/3 cup + 2 tbsp. ruby red grapefruit juice (100 mL)

2 tbsp. cassis (25 mL)

2 oz. bittersweet chocolate (60 g), melted

2 large ruby red grapefruit,
   peeled and cut between membranes

To make the crust, preheat oven to 325°F. Butter eight 3-inch (8 cm) tartlet moulds that are about 1 inch (2.5 cm) deep.

Combine all the crust ingredients with your hands until blended. Divide the crust mixture evenly among tart moulds. Press the crust firmly into the bottom and up the sides of each mould. Place on a cookie sheet and bake for 10 to 13 minutes, or until golden and crisp. Tarts will puff up when ready. Remove from oven and poke gently with a fork to deflate. Cool for about 10 minutes. Remove shells from moulds.

In a large stainless steel bowl or the top of a double boiler, whisk together the sabayon ingredients. Place over a pot of gently simmering water. Whisk vigorously until sabayon becomes thick and forms ribbons when whisk is lifted, 7 to 9 minutes. Remove bowl from heat.

To assemble the tarts, spread about 1 1/2 tsp. (7 mL) melted chocolate in the bottom of each tart shell. Let cool slightly. Divide the sabayon equally among tart shells and top with sections of fresh grapefruit. Serve immediately.

MAKES 8 TARTS

pistachio hazelnut baklava

I finally broke down and developed a recipe for baklava. Usually, I find it so darn sweet, but this one is done my way. I also changed the traditional walnuts to a combo of pistachios and hazelnuts. After being slow-cooked, the nuts, sugar and phyllo just melt in your mouth. I shape these as little blossoms for visual effect, but you can also make them in the traditional cigar shape.

1/3 cup raw pistachios (75 mL)

1/4 cup whole hazelnuts (60 mL), toasted and skinned

pinch ground cloves

1/4 cup + 2 tbsp. sugar (60 mL + 25 mL)

2 tsp. + 1/2 tsp. cinnamon (10 mL + 2 mL)

6 sheets phyllo

1/4 cup melted unsalted butter (60 mL)

1/4 cup water (60 mL)

1/4 cup amber Greek honey or other good-quality honey (60 mL)

1 tbsp. lemon juice (15 mL)

Preheat oven to 325°F. Line a baking sheet with parchment paper.

In a food processor, combine the pistachios, hazelnuts, cloves, 1/4 cup (60 mL) of the sugar and 2 tsp. (10 mL) of the cinnamon. Pulse until nuts are coarsely chopped. Set aside.

In a small bowl, stir together the remaining 2 tbsp. (25 mL) sugar and 1/2 tsp. (2 mL) cinnamon.

Lay out 1 sheet of phyllo (keep remaining phyllo under a damp tea towel) and brush gently with some melted butter. Sprinkle with a little of the cinnamon sugar. Lay another piece of phyllo on top and repeat the brushing and sprinkling, ending with a layer of phyllo that is not brushed with butter.

Cut the phyllo into thirds in both directions, creating 9 rectangles. Place about 1 tbsp. (15 mL) of the nut filling in the middle of each rectangle. Gather up the corners of each rectangle and pinch together to create a little bundle.

Transfer bundles to baking sheet and bake for 35 to 40 minutes, or until browned and crisp. Let cool completely on the baking sheet. Transfer baklava to a baking dish just large enough to hold them.

Meanwhile, combine water, honey and lemon juice in a small saucepan. Bring to a boil, stirring, and remove from heat. Pour over cooled baklava and let stand 30 to 90 minutes before serving for best flavour.

MAKES 9 PIECES

lemon cheese strudel

I had this interesting strudel on my pastry menu at Toronto's Scaramouche restaurant. It's a cross between a cheesecake and a lemon Danish. The blueberry cinnamon sauce is a brilliant accompaniment.

BLUEBERRY CINNAMON SAUCE

2 cups fresh or frozen blueberries (500 mL)

1/4 cup sugar (60 mL)

1 tbsp. cornstarch (15 mL)

juice of 1/2 lemon

1 cinnamon stick

2 thin slices fresh ginger

LEMON CURD

3 egg yolks

1/4 cup sugar (60 mL)

1/4 cup lemon juice (60 mL)

grated zest of 1 lemon

1 lb. cream cheese (500 g), at room temperature

1/4 cup icing sugar (60 mL), plus additional for garnish

1 egg

6 sheets phyllo

1/3 cup melted butter (75 mL)

granulated sugar, for sprinkling

To make the sauce, combine all sauce ingredients in a medium saucepan and bring to a boil, stirring constantly. Reduce heat to low and simmer 2 to 3 minutes, or until sauce is a syrupy consistency. Remove from heat and discard the ginger and cinnamon stick. Set aside.

To make the lemon curd, in the top of a double boiler or in a small stainless steel bowl, whisk together egg yolks, sugar, lemon juice and zest. Set over gently simmering water and whisk for 7 to 10 minutes, or until thickened. Remove from heat and cover surface with plastic wrap. Chill for at least 30 minutes.

Preheat oven to 375°F. Line a baking sheet with parchment paper.

Combine cream cheese and icing sugar in a medium bowl. With an electric mixer, beat on medium speed until light and creamy. Add the egg and the chilled lemon curd. Beat on medium speed just until well blended.

Lay a sheet of phyllo on a surface with the long end facing you. (Keep remaining phyllo under a damp tea towel.) Brush with melted butter. Lay another sheet on top, and continue brushing and layering.

Pour cream cheese filling lengthwise along the phyllo, creating a log about 6 inches (15 cm) from the edge facing you and leaving a border 1 1/2 inches (4 cm) on each side. Roll the strudel away from you, turning once. Fold sides over, securing well, and fold strudel over into thirds. Strudel should be about 3 inches (8 cm) thick.

Transfer the strudel to the baking sheet, seam side down. Sprinkle with granulated sugar and cut two small slits in top of phyllo for steam to escape. Bake for 17 to 20 minutes, or until golden and puffed. Let cool slightly before serving.

Meanwhile, reheat the sauce.

Sprinkle strudel with icing sugar and serve drizzled with warm blueberry sauce.

SERVES 8

raspberry kiwi pavlova

You'll get great technical marks from the Russian judge for making this New Zealand–inspired dessert — it was actually named for a Russian ballerina. The meringue should be just golden and crisp, but still gooey in the centre like a marshmallow. I love making this dessert in the winter when the weather is dry and crisp. Humidity and meringues don't get along.

4 egg whites, at room temperature	2 tbsp. corn flour (25 mL)
pinch salt	1 tbsp. apple cider vinegar (15 mL)
1/4 tsp. cream of tartar (1 mL)	1/2 tsp. vanilla (2 mL)
3/4 cup sugar (175 mL)	

Preheat oven to 350°F. Line a baking sheet with parchment paper.

In a large clean stainless steel bowl, beat egg whites and salt with an electric beater on high speed until peaks just start to form. Beat in the cream of tartar, then gradually beat in the sugar in a slow stream. Beat until stiff peaks form and meringue is glossy, 3 to 4 minutes. Gently fold in the corn flour, vinegar and vanilla until well blended.

Spoon the meringue onto the baking sheet. Using the back of a spoon, spread the mixture into a 9-inch (23 cm) circle, building the edge up slightly higher than the middle.

Bake for 20 minutes. Reduce temperature to 200°F and bake for a further 30 minutes, or until the pavlova is just golden. Turn oven off and let the pavlova cool in the oven for 1 hour or until dry and crisp on the outside. It should still be soft on the inside.

RASPBERRY AND KIWI COMPOTE	1 cup late-harvest wine (250 mL)
3 cups raspberries (750 mL)	1 tbsp. sugar (15 mL)
juice of 1/2 lemon	2 kiwis, peeled and diced

In a medium saucepan, combine half of the raspberries, the lemon juice, wine and sugar. Bring to a boil on high heat, stirring. Reduce heat to low and simmer, uncovered, until reduced by half. Strain the mixture into a medium bowl, pressing on the berries. Let cool completely. Stir in the rest of the raspberries and the kiwi.

Just before serving, spoon compote mixture all over the pavlova.

SERVES 8

spicy maple pumpkin pie

I get more requests for a good pumpkin pie recipe than for any other, except maybe my lemon meringue pie. I add a touch of cayenne to the filling for an extra kick.

PASTRY

1 1/3 cups all-purpose flour (325 mL)

pinch salt

1/3 cup cold vegetable shortening (75 mL)

1/4 cup cold unsalted butter (60 mL), cut into pieces

1/3 cup ice water (75 mL)

Preheat the oven to 375°F.

Sift together the flour and salt. With a pastry cutter or two knives, blend in the shortening and butter until the mixture resembles coarse crumbs. Add the ice water gradually, stirring with a fork until dough forms. Pat the dough into a disk, wrap in plastic wrap and refrigerate for at least 1 hour.

On a lightly floured surface, roll the dough into a 13-inch (33 cm) round. Place it in a 9-inch (23 cm) pie plate and crimp the edges in a decorative pattern. Pierce the bottom with a fork. Place a piece of parchment or foil in the shell. Fill the shell with pie weights or dried beans. Bake for 20 minutes. Remove the pie weights and paper and bake another 20 to 25 minutes, or until the pastry is golden and crisp. Cool on a wire rack.

FILLING

1 can (14 oz./398 mL) pure pumpkin purée

2 eggs, lightly beaten

1/2 cup brown sugar (125 mL)

1/2 cup whipping (35%) cream (125 mL)

2 tbsp. sour cream (25 mL)

2 tbsp. maple syrup (25 mL)

1 tsp. ground ginger (5 mL)

1/4 tsp. ground allspice (1 mL)

1/4 tsp. freshly grated nutmeg (1 mL)

pinch ground cloves

pinch cayenne

whipped cream, for garnish

Preheat oven to 325°F.

Combine all filling ingredients in a medium bowl and whisk to blend well. Pour filling into cooled pie shell. Bake for 25 to 30 minutes, or until filling is set but a spot in the middle the size of quarter is still soft. Let cool completely.

Serve pie with dollops of whipped cream.

SERVES 8

lemon-lime soufflé tart

Obviously I have a thing for lemons! This tart features a super-tangy, fluffy filling that contrasts with its spicy ginger crust. To save time, the crust can be made ahead and frozen.

GINGER CRUST

1 1/2 cups all-purpose flour (375 mL)

1/2 cup cold butter (125 mL), cut into pieces

1/3 cup icing sugar (75 mL)

1 tsp. grated fresh ginger (5 mL)

1/8 tsp. ground cloves (1 mL)

1/4 tsp. cinnamon (2 mL)

pinch salt

1 egg

2 tbsp. molasses (25 mL)

LEMON-LIME FILLING

1/3 cup + 2 tbsp. sugar (75 mL + 25 mL)

1/3 cup mixed lemon and lime juice (75 mL)

1/4 cup whipping (35%) cream (60 mL)

grated zest of 1 lemon

2 eggs, separated

To make the crust, combine flour, butter, sugar, ginger, cloves, cinnamon and salt in a food processor. Pulse until mixture resembles coarse meal. Lightly beat egg with molasses and add to flour mixture while pulsing machine. Pulse several times until dough comes together. Turn out dough and knead into a ball. Cover and refrigerate for at least 30 minutes.

Preheat oven to 350°F.

On a well-floured surface, roll out dough to a 12-inch (30 cm) round. Line a 9-inch (23 cm) fluted flan ring (2 inches/5 cm deep) with the pastry, pressing sides down to secure. Roll a rolling pin across the flan ring to trim away overhang. Prick the pastry all over with a fork and freeze for 10 minutes.

Bake tart shell for 30 to 35 minutes, or until golden. (Since pastry is cookie-like it does not need to be "baked blind" with beans.) If the shell puffs up, just poke down gently with a fork. Let shell cool completely in the ring, about 45 minutes.

Preheat oven to 325°F.

To make the filling, in a medium bowl, whisk together 1/3 cup (75 mL) of the sugar, the lemon and lime juice, cream, lemon zest and egg yolks. In a separate bowl with an electric mixer, whip egg whites on high speed. When soft peaks form, slowly add the remaining 2 tbsp. (25 mL) sugar. Continue to beat on high for 1 to 2 minutes, or until whites are glossy and stiff.

Gently fold egg whites into lemon-lime filling, ensuring that all whites are well incorporated but being careful not to deflate the egg whites.

Place tart shell on the middle rack of the oven and pour in the filling. Tart should be filled to the very top of the shell. Be careful not to spill filling over the edge. Bake for 25 minutes, or until middle of tart is just firm when jiggled.

Cool tart slightly and serve warm.

SERVES 12

super-crispy free-form apple pie

This is one of those pies that I have been making for years but never really had a recipe for. Thanks for making me put it on paper. The pastry is an adaptation of Jacques Pepin's, with a completely different procedure. I use a pastry scraper and a rolling pin to create a rough — almost — puff pastry. Cutting the butter in ultra-thin slices creates great crispy layers. The firm, tart and crisp Mutsu apple is my choice for the best apple pie, but you could also use Gala, Spy or Granny Smith.

PASTRY

1 3/4 cups all-purpose flour (425 mL)

1/3 cup cake-and-pastry flour (75 mL)

1/4 tsp. salt (1 mL)

3/4 cup cold butter (175 mL), cut into very thin slices

1/2 cup ice water (125 mL)

1 egg, lightly beaten

1 tbsp. sugar (15 mL)

FILLING

4 large Mutsu (Crispin) or other firm cooking apples

juice of 1/2 lemon

1/3 cup sugar (75 mL)

1 tbsp. cornstarch (15 mL)

1/2 tsp. cinnamon (2 mL)

ground allspice to taste

To make the pastry, in a medium bowl, stir together the all-purpose flour, cake-and-pastry flour, salt and butter with a spatula. Do not break up the slices of butter. Slowly add the water while tossing the flour mixture until water is absorbed. Turn mixture onto a lightly floured surface. Pastry should still be messy.

Do not touch the dough with your hands. Instead, use a rolling pin and a pastry scraper or spatula to gently knead the dough together. Roll the dough with a rolling pin. Use the scraper to fold the outer edges back onto the dough. Working quickly so butter does not get soft, continue to roll and fold the dough, creating layers, until the butter is evenly incorporated. Divide dough in half. Using the rolling pin, flatten into 2 disks. Wrap the dough in plastic wrap and refrigerate for 45 minutes.

Meanwhile, make the apple filling. Quarter the apples and thinly slice them. In a large bowl, toss apples with lemon juice. Add remaining filling ingredients; toss together.

Preheat oven to 375°F. Line a baking sheet with parchment paper.

On a lightly floured surface, roll 1 disk of dough into an 11-inch (28 cm) circle. Transfer circle to the baking sheet. Brush pastry all over with beaten egg. Mound the filling onto the middle of pastry, discarding any liquid in bottom of bowl. Roll out remaining dough into a 10-inch (25 cm) circle. Place over filling and press edges together to seal tightly. Fold edge over again towards middle of pie and pinch decoratively between the folds. Press down around edges so there are no gaps. Brush the top of the pastry with beaten egg and sprinkle very lightly with sugar.

Cut a 1/2-inch (1 cm) hole in the middle of the pastry. Cut a few more steam holes in the top of the pastry.

Bake on the lower rack for 45 to 50 minutes, or until pastry is crisp and golden and filling is bubbly. If the pastry gets too dark and the filling is not bubbly, reduce heat to 350°F for the final 15 minutes of baking.

SERVES 10 TO 12

lip-smacking lemon meringue pie

Everyone who tries this pie wants the recipe. I suggest you follow the directions to the T because meringues can be a pain in the ... As always when I am making meringue, I make sure the bowl is super clean. I also use a whisk attachment, and I only begin to very gradually add the sugar once the egg whites have begun to form peaks.

PASTRY

1 1/3 cups all-purpose flour (325 mL)

pinch salt

1/3 cup cold vegetable shortening (75 mL)

1/4 cup cold unsalted butter (60 mL), cut into pieces

1/3 cup ice water (75 mL)

Preheat oven to 375°F.

Sift together the flour and salt. With a pastry cutter or two knives, blend in the shortening and butter until the mixture resembles coarse crumbs. Add the ice water gradually, stirring with a fork until dough forms. Pat the dough into a disk, wrap in plastic wrap and refrigerate for at least 1 hour.

On a lightly floured surface, roll the dough into a 13-inch (33 cm) round. Place it in a 9-inch (23 cm) pie plate and crimp the edges in a decorative pattern. Pierce the bottom with a fork. Place a piece of parchment or foil in the shell and fill with dried beans or pie weights. Bake for 20 minutes. Remove the paper and pie weights and bake another 20 to 25 minutes, or until the pastry is golden and crisp. Cool on a wire rack while you make the lemon curd.

LEMON CURD

2/3 cup cornstarch (150 mL)

2 cups water (500 mL)

10 egg yolks

1 1/3 cup sugar (325 mL)

1 cup lemon juice (250 mL)

grated zest of 4 lemons

pinch salt

In a small bowl, whisk the cornstarch with 1 cup (250 mL) of the water until dissolved. Set aside. In a small saucepan, whisk together egg yolks, sugar, lemon juice, lemon zest, salt and the remaining 1 cup (250 mL) water. Cook over medium-low heat for 1 minute, stirring constantly, until sugar has dissolved. Do not let the mixture boil.

Pour in the cornstarch mixture and increase heat to medium. Cook mixture, stirring constantly with a wooden spoon so that the mixture does not stick to the bottom or the sides of the pan, until it starts to boil, thickens and becomes translucent, 6 to 8 minutes. Remove from heat and let cool slightly.

Preheat oven to 375°F. Immediately make meringue.

MERINGUE
4 egg whites
1/2 tsp. cream of tartar (2 mL)
1/2 cup sugar (125 mL)

With an electric mixer, beat egg whites on high speed. When frothy, add cream of tartar and beat until soft peaks begin to form. While beating, sprinkle in half of the sugar in a very slow stream. When peaks begin to stiffen, beat in remaining sugar in a steady stream until peaks are shiny and stiff.

Pour the warm filling into the cooled pie shell and spread the meringue on top, making sure to reach the edges of the pastry. Use a spatula to swirl the meringue into peaks. Bake pie for 6 minutes, or until meringue is just golden.

Serve pie at room temperature.

SERVES 8 TO 10

soft sticky cinnamon buns

It seems as if I've spent years trying to make the perfect cinnamon bun, a bun this soft and tender in the middle and not too sweet. This recipe has taken many years to perfect, but I think you'll love it. The potato makes the dough tender, but it's a little unpredictable: how much moisture the potato contains will dictate how much flour you need. I suggest you keep adding flour until the dough is satiny and smooth. I bake the potato instead of boiling it because it absorbs way too much water when it's boiled.

8 oz. Yukon Gold potato (250 g)

1/3 cup + 1/4 cup sugar (75 mL + 60 mL)

3 tbsp. + 2 tbsp. melted butter (45 mL + 25 mL)

1 pkg. active dry yeast

1/2 cup warm milk (125 mL)

1 egg, beaten

3/4 tsp. salt (4 mL)

2 1/2 cups all-purpose flour (625 mL)

1/2 cup finely chopped pecans (125 mL)

2 tsp. cinnamon (10 mL)

pinch ground allspice

GLAZE

1/2 cup icing sugar (125 mL)

1/4 cup maple syrup (60 mL)

2 tbsp. orange juice (25 mL)

1/2 tsp. cinnamon (2 mL)

Preheat oven to 400°F. Poke holes all over potato and bake until tender, about 50 minutes. Peel immediately and mash. Spread out on a plate to cool and set aside.

Meanwhile, in a large bowl stir together 1/4 cup (60 mL) of the sugar and 3 tbsp. (45 mL) of the melted butter. In a small bowl, stir the yeast into the warm milk; let stand until foaming, about 5 minutes.

Add the yeast and mashed potato to the butter mixture. Stir with a wooden spoon to blend. Add egg and salt; stir until well blended. Add 2 cups (500 mL) of the flour and stir with a wooden spoon until dough comes together.

Turn onto a lightly floured surface and knead for 8 to 10 minutes, adding more flour as needed. Dough should be smooth and satiny, and slightly tacky but not sticky to the touch.

Transfer dough to a large oiled bowl. Cover and let sit in a warm place until doubled in bulk, about 1 hour.

Punch down dough. On a lightly floured piece of parchment paper, roll dough out to a 10 1/2- by 15-inch (26 cm by 38 cm) rectangle. Turn rectangle so a long side faces you. Brush dough with remaining 2 tbsp. (25 mL) melted butter.

In a small bowl, stir together remaining 1/3 cup (75 mL) sugar, the pecans, cinnamon and allspice. Sprinkle mixture evenly over dough. Roll dough tightly away from you like a jelly roll.

Line a jelly roll pan with parchment paper.

Cut roll with a serrated knife into 12 equal slices about 1 1/4 inches (3 cm) thick. Transfer to jelly roll pan, leaving about 1/2 inch (1 cm) between buns. Cover loosely with tea towel and let rise in a warm place until nearly doubled, about 45 minutes.

Meanwhile, preheat oven to 375°F.

Brush buns with a little melted butter. Bake for 20 to 25 minutes, or until buns are golden on top and bottoms are browned. Let cool in the pan.

To make the glaze, in a small saucepan, combine sugar, maple syrup, orange juice and cinnamon. Heat, without stirring, until just boiling. Let cool slightly.

Brush cooled buns with glaze.

MAKES 12 BUNS

lemon crème brûlée tarts with chocolate shortbread crust

I have to tell you, this method of making crème brûlée yields the silkiest possible custard. It's a little more time-consuming because you have to stand and stir the custard, but you won't believe how smooth it is. These tarts are meant to be eaten as soon as you fill them and caramelize the tops. When we tested these tarts, we stopped counting how many we ate.

CHOCOLATE SHORTBREAD CRUST
1 egg
1/3 cup icing sugar (75 mL)
1 1/4 cups all-purpose flour (300 mL)
1/4 cup cocoa powder (60 mL)
pinch salt
1/2 cup cold butter (125 mL)

In a small bowl, whisk the egg and sugar until smooth, about 2 minutes. Sift flour, cocoa and salt into a food processor. Add the butter and pulse until mixture resembles fine cornmeal. Add egg mixture and pulse until dough comes together. Do not overwork. Shape dough into a disk. Cover with plastic and refrigerate for at least 30 minutes.

Preheat oven to 350°F. Have ready 24 tartlet moulds (approx. 2 inches/5 cm wide).

On a floured surface, roll dough into a round about 1/8 inch (3 mm) thick. Cut circles with cookie cutters or top of glass 1 inch (2.5 cm) larger than the tart moulds. Line the moulds, pressing pastry in evenly and firmly. Poke with a fork and freeze for about 10 minutes. Place moulds on a baking sheet and bake on bottom rack of oven for 15 minutes, or until firm and crisp. Let cool.

FILLING

1 cup whipping (35%) cream (250 mL)

3 tbsp. sugar (45 mL)

3 egg yolks

2 tbsp. lemon juice (25 mL)

grated zest of 1/2 lemon

2 tbsp. butter (25 mL)

1/4 tsp. vanilla (1 mL)

3 tbsp. sugar (45 mL), for caramelizing tops of tarts

Bring water in a saucepan or the bottom of a double boiler to a gentle simmer. Bring cream and sugar to a boil in a small saucepan, stirring until sugar is melted. In a medium stainless steel bowl or top of a double boiler, whisk together the yolks, lemon juice and zest. While whisking, pour hot cream into yolk mixture and whisk to blend. Place the cream mixture over simmering water and stir constantly with a wooden spoon until mixture thickens and heavily coats the back of the spoon, 20 to 25 minutes.

Strain filling through a sieve. Stir in butter and vanilla. Cover surface with plastic wrap and chill for at least 2 hours.

Just before serving, fill tart shells with filling. Sprinkle each shell with sugar to cover surface. Caramelize the sugar with a small blowtorch or under a broiler.

MAKES 24 TARTS

index